Food Security & Sustainability For the Times Ahead

Also by
Harvest McCampbell

Sacred Smoke

Out of Print:
Life is a Gift
Women's Health Begins with the Moon
Finding Your Way with Herbs

Up Coming:
One Day at a Time in the Garden

Food Security

&

Sustainability

For the Times Ahead

Harvest McCampbell

Bio Diverse Press

www.BioDiversePress.com

Food Security & Sustainability, For the Times Ahead

Design and Photography: Harvest McCampbell, except where otherwise noted. Photos on pages 4 & 97 previously appeared in the Hoopa People Newspaper, which has now been renamed—The Two Rivers Tribune.

Editing: Terri Holtzclaw Reiser, Sal Camarillo

Bio Diverse Press

www.BioDiversePress.com

biodiversepress@ymail.com

Publisher's Cataloging-in Publication data

McCampbell, Harvest.

Food security & sustainability for the times ahead / Harvest McCampbell.

p. cm.

ISBN 978-0-9818975-0-9

Includes bibliographical references and index.

1. Food--Storage. 2. Food--Preservation. 3. Emergency food supply. 4. Survival skills. 5. Survival and emergency equipment. I. Food security and sustainability for the times ahead. II. Title.

TX601 .M27 2008

641.4 20--dc22 20088933399

Legal Disclaimer:

This book contains information about food security, sustainability, and disaster preparedness. It is intended to encourage people to do more research, think for themselves, and be prepared. Neither the author nor the publisher is to be held liable for any possible negative outcomes from these practices.

Notes on Reference Citations:

Outside references are enclosed in "quotation marks," unless they are books, in which case they are in *italics*. Web addresses are <bracketed>. When other parts of this book are referenced, chapter titles are listed in **bold**, section and subsection headings are in ***bold italic***.

Dedicated to
All regional food movements
Organic gardeners and farmers
And those striving to live
Greener lives

Together we will change the world

Contents

Introduction, by T'Uy'Tanat-Cease Wyss 8
Author's Foreword, Food Security & the Green World 10
1. Stories of the Green World 13
2. Transition 15
3. The Times Ahead 19
4. Sustainability 21
5. Food Security 101 23
6. Location, Location, Location 26
7. Storing Staples Securely 31
Shelf Life . . . 32 Insects, Rodents, & Bears . . . 33
Earthquakes, Hurricanes, & Tornadoes . . . 35
High Rainfall or Humidity . . . 36
Flooding; Fire; Heat & Light . . . 37
Rancidity, Physical Hazards, Ethics . . . 38
Storage Space, Storage Containers . . . 39
Labeling, Sealing Your Containers . . . 40
8. Wise Food Choices for Storage 42
Canned Goods . . . 42
Packaged Snacks, Pasta, Powdered Milk and Eggs, Nuts . . . 43
Water, Whole Grains and Dry Beans . . . 44
9. Poor Choices for Food Storage 45
Low Nutritional Value, High Moisture Content . . . 45
Crushable, Packaged in Cardboard, Refrigerated or Frozen . . . 46
Flour and Baking Mixes . . . 47
10. Balance is Everything 48
Complex Carbohydrates . . . 48
Protein; Fat; Dietary Fiber; Calcium . . . 49
Anti-oxidants, Phyto-nutrients, Vitamins, and Minerals . . . 50
Vitamin B 12 . . . 50 Water, Water, Water . . . 51
11. Process Your Own Fats and Oils 52
Animal Fat . . . 52 Vegetable Oil . . . 54
12. Shop Flexible, Shop Wise 56
13. Don't Forget Your Immune System 58
Vitamin C . . . 58 Garlic . . . 59
Echinacea, Cayenne and Chili Peppers . . . 60
Shiitake Mushrooms, Oregon Grape . . . 61
Salt . . . 62
Local Medicinal Plants, General Herb Information . . . 64

14. Other Essential Herbs 66
American Ephedra, Cleavers . . . 66
Comfrey, Mint, Mullein, Fennel, White Willow . . . 67
Yellow Dock, Yerba Santa , Herbal Preparations . . . 68
Medicinal Actions . . . 69 Wild Crafting, Herb Safety . . . 70
Herbs by Mail Order . . . 70 More Information . . . 71
15. Additional Items for Emergency Caches 72
16. Forget About Guns 76
17. Your Food Storage Plan 78
18. Packing the Emergency Cache 82
19. Food Security and the Garden 85
20. Old Time Food Preservation and Storage 89
Root Cellars, Spring Houses . . . 89
Fermentation, Drying and Dehydrating, More Information . . . 90
21. Gram, The Green World, Oxygen & Water 92
Oxygen . . . 93 Water . . . 94
Water filtering, Water Development . . . 96
22. Useful Skills 97
Basket Weaving, Bee Keeping, Birth Control . . . 99
Canning & Dehydrating . . . 100
Composting, Cordage, Fire Making . . . 101
Gourd Growing and Crafting, Hide Tanning . . . 102
Primitive Ceramics, Seed Saving, Soap making . . . 103
Spinning, Weaving, Crochet, & Knitting . . . 104
Traditional & Alternative Building, Farming, Food Preservation . . 105
Traditional & Primitive Tool Making, Vinegar Making . . . 106
Waste Management, Water Witching or Dousing . . . 107
Whittling and Wood Carving . . . 107
Wild Foods & Medicines . . . 108
23. So You Want To Be An Apprentice? 109
24. Each One Teach One 112
25. Rethinking Economies and Careers 115
26. Take Time to Reflect 117
27. More Resources 119
On the Web . . . 119 Advocacy and Action, Gardening . . . 120
Learn More, News, Recommended Reading . . . 121
Sources for Gardeners . . . 124 Educational Opportunities . . . 126
About the Author, by Jessica Palmer 128
Acknowledgments 131
Bio Diverse Press 134
Recycle this Book 135
Index 136

INTRODUCTION

By T'Uy'Tanat-Cease Wyss

In my work as the Food Enhancement Coordinator with Vancouver Native Health Society, I have the opportunity to look over many books and articles that might benefit our clients. *Food Security and Sustainability for the Times Ahead* is one of the most significant titles on the subject in print today. Harvest McCampbell takes simple and sensible teachings about food security and sustainability, which were once common household knowledge, and combines them with modern resources and research skills. She shares it all in a short book that can easily fit into anyone's mindset.

It is refreshing to read a book of this nature in contemporary times, as we are being fed the "disposable society diet," which leaves our spirits, minds, and our bodies without much hope for a long and healthy life. This book is a remarkably easy read. It makes planning for disasters, temporary emergencies, peak oil, and climate change much less intimidating. It empowers the reader and reminds us not to get side tracked by theories that the world may end sooner than we think. She shows us, very calmly, that we are capable of surviving, healthily and in style, without the capitalist society to support us.

Much of the book is based on information that Harvest learned from her grandmother—who was born in the late 1800's. Harvest has a knack for making the reader feel like they are right by her side, back in the day, listening to Gram's stories. Gram made certain that her words were carefully stored, like a healthy cache of food and supplies, in her young granddaughter's mind.

This is a wonderful book. It not only gives you the facts and ideas for your own personal Food Security Plan in a truly sustainable way, it is like having a mini-life skills course on survival, with the personal touch of conversational writing. As Harvest shares in this book, the best way to keep these traditional and sustainable skills intact is to use them, and use them regularly.

I know this: I wouldn't want to be caught in an emergency without even a quarter of what I have learned here. Although there are many survivalist type books out there, there are very few, if any, who offer such easy advice and promote a sense of well being for their readers in their efforts to encourage personal survival and sustainability. This book is a very realistic and non-intimidating.

On a personal note, Harvest and I have been sharing teachings, those from my own traditions and life and those from hers, for close to a decade and a half. We have enjoyed this on-going series of stories that have entered Harvest's writing, my film making, and my current work as a food security professional. This cross pollination has nourished our personal growth and our efforts to be food secure in modern times. The goal has always been to be as autonomous as possible; this book will get you all the way there.

T'Uy'Tanat-Cease Wyss
"Woman who travels by canoe to gather Medicines for all People"

Program Coordinator
Urban Aboriginal Food Enhancement Program
& Cultural Coordinator
Urban Aboriginal Community Kitchen Garden Project
Vancouver Native Health Society
<http://www.vnhs.net>

Ceasefire Productions & Senaqwila Herbal Tea Company
<http://www.technomedicinehweel.org>

Author's Foreword

Food Security & the Green World

In the winter of 2008, a number of news reports claimed that the jet stream was "on steroids." I began doing some research on the jet stream, as well as other topics presented in these news articles. La Nina, ocean currents, ocean temperature anomalies, and the melting ice sheets in Antarctica were all connected. As I continued to read, I came across massive flood warnings for the Midwest, and news of crop failures and food shortages around the world. I also began finding other stories that claimed that the fall of Western Civilization was looming. My grandmother's old stories began to creep into my dreams.

During this time I was working on another manuscript, *One Day at a Time in the Garden, a Recovery Plan for the Planet.* It is an ambitious project, with an entry for every day of the year. I began to think that I might be too late. Perhaps the infrastructure necessary for book publishing would collapse before I was finished. Writing requires discipline, discipline requires commitment, and commitment requires a vision of the future. My vision of the future was faltering. What welled up in its place was a vision of the Green World that my grandmother had described to me, long ago.

I made an effort to get my community interested in food security. I found that few people were willing to read the writing on the wall;

even when that writing came from organizations like the National Weather Service, the National Oceanic and Atmospheric Administration, and the New York Times. Those who would listen explained that it was too scary for most people to think about, so they just tuned me out. By this time I had stopped working on my gardening book, and I was feeling very frustrated.

My friend and assistant, Jessica Palmer, then suggested that I write a book on food security. I looked at her askance, and she added, "A little book, it doesn't have to be 400 pages long." It took me a few weeks to get started, and only six weeks to finish the rough draft, while the Midwest suffered through the worst flooding in recorded history. (Over five million agricultural acres were inundated.) The polishing process has taken longer and much more of my attention. Please forgive any errors, my editors and I have been in a hurry to get this book out.

During the editing phase, Eastern Humboldt County, where I live, has been declared in a State of Emergency, because of hazardous air quality. We had an unprecedented early dry lightning storm that sparked over 1,000 fires here in Northern and Central California. These fires burned nearly 1,000,000 acres, as of July, 2008. (They are still burning as I write and edit.) The intensity and extent of the fires is blamed on climate change and global warming. Many people have left the area. The rest of us are urged to stay indoors, to keep the air conditioners or air filters running, or to visit a clean air facility during the day. Looking on the bright side, it is good weather for writing and editing, but I grieve for those once green hills and canyons. I hear the effects of the fire and smoke will have a large impact on California's agricultural year. It really is time for us to focus, as families and individuals, on our personal food security.

While this book was written with a North American audience in mind, anyone who reads English and has the luxury of stocking up on staples will benefit from the information. Please keep in mind that stocking up is a luxury beyond the dreams of many people living in third world countries. Food security for these people is also very much on my mind. You will see that some of the advice in this book addresses our influence on the supply and cost of food. We can improve everyone's food security while we improve our own, if we are careful and thoughtful.

I hope, as one of my editors, Terri Reiser, noted repeatedly in the margins of the draft, "This will save lives." I hope the book will help you weather the changes ahead. Most of all, I hope this book will bring you closer to earth, to family and friends, to the Green World of my grandmother's dreams.

1. Stories of the Green World

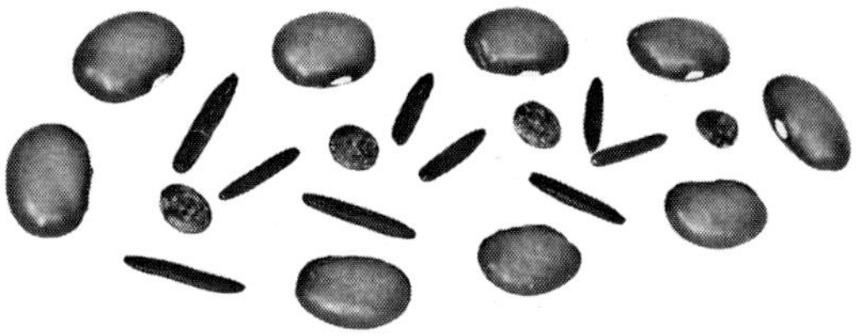

A long time ago, when I was a little girl, I loved tagging along with my grandmother. Gram was born in the late 1800's, when the world was very different than it is today. Even for her time, she was an unusual and highly gifted woman. She told me stories of the old days, and the days that are to come. Some of these stories she considered secret; they were, at that time, just between Gram and me. Mom and my aunties didn't think Gram was doing me any favors with her stories and teachings. But Gram's stories were compelling, and no matter what my other relatives had to say, I always listened.

Grandmother was of mixed ancestry, primarily Northern European and Native American (as are most of my close ancestors). She followed a branch of the Ghost Dance Religion, and believed that one day all the cement and asphalt would disappear. On that day we would have our Green World back. That world, Gram told me, would be very much like North America was—a thousand years ago.

We would often gather herbs and wild foods that grew out in the woods, where there was no sign of human activity. She would say, "Maybe today, maybe when we get back to where we left the car, there will be no car, there will be no roads. Then what will we do Little One?" I was expected to come up with a plan. Not in a vacuum, of course.

Gram spent the last years of her life teaching me how to survive in that Green World. I was prompted to come up with a plan, based on all she had taught me about surviving in the woods and living off the land. "What are we going to eat, Child?" She would ask, "What will we use for medicine if we get sick?"

I spent many years of my life practicing, teaching, and writing—about what Gram taught me. Whenever I wandered out of sight of the artifacts of the cement and asphalt civilization, I wondered, I actually hoped, "Maybe today?" After a few decades passed, I became very busy with my life, and eventually quit thinking about my grandmother's Green World.

The news is now full of gloom. Climate change, earthquakes, massive storms, and crop failures are featured nearly daily. Reading this news has brought what Grandmother taught me back to mind. She taught me to live gently on our mother, the earth. While she never used the word "sustainable," she was all about its meaning. She embraced the idea of living in harmony with creation, with the seasons, and with the landscapes we inhabit. She taught me to take only what was needed, and to always leave enough for the next family, for the next generation, for the eons of life that should follow us. All living things were sacred in her eyes, including the insects who shared our garden, and the frogs who fed on the insects—insuring that we would also have a share.

Ignoring nature's need for balance has brought us to the gloomy state of our current news. Perhaps it is time for a transition away from the values of greed back to something much more sustainable and harmonious.

2. Transition

I do believe we will have our Green World back. Unfortunately, I don't think it will be as simple as waking up one morning and discovering that all the asphalt and cement are gone. I believe there is a transition involved, and that it has already begun.

Change is hard, and this transition is already filled with difficult times: weather patterns are shifting, catastrophic floods and fires are more common, storms are increasing in intensity and frequency, earthquakes and volcanic eruptions are becoming more prevalent. Many people have already died and many more are suffering. Our food supplies are increasingly insecure. Unaware, most of us depend on huge agribusiness corporations for our food. While this unsustainable system was somewhat efficient in feeding the world when the weather was fairly predictable, that is changing.

Pick up any newspaper, on almost any day of the week, and you will find news about food: rising prices, crop failures, food shortages, starvation, and riots. Meanwhile, those who have tons of money are doing what they have always done—they use it to make more money. The very wealthy are outbidding each other on whole crops, causing the prices to rise even further. The poorest people on the planet are getting priced out of a place at the world's dinner table, while the rich are getting richer. (See "Food, Fuel, and Economic Crises News," in the ***On the Web*** section, Chapter 27, **More Resources**.)

We now have 14,000 times more carbon in our atmosphere than ever. It doesn't appear that this trend is slowing down any time soon. Developing nations, the United States, and third world countries continue to pour out carbon at ever increasing rates. The trees that could pull the carbon out of our air are cut down, and our weather has goes wild. Meanwhile, glaciers and ice sheets are melting; which jeopardizes water supplies and ocean currents.

The initial view seems horrendous, but I believe there is hope. Nature has a plan. Reforestation is the key to reducing carbon. Trees breathe in carbon and exhale oxygen. Everywhere I walk, I see tree seeds piling up and blowing around. Tree seeds have found their way into my vegetable starts and taken root. A friend of mine has oak trees sprouting all over her property; where there were never oaks before. Take a look around you, you will find tree seeds and seedlings working on nature's reforestation plan. The trees will heal the planet. It is going to take time. We have to be patient and cooperate. We have to do our part and educate others. And we must prepare to weather the transition.

Until the transition to the Green World is complete, we are going to have to live in both worlds at the same time. We may need to keep up our obligations to the industrial and corporate world; while at the same time, we must strive to provide our families with good quality food from our gardens or from small organic farms. This may sound like too much work or expense, but it is truly necessary to weather the transition.

This is not the first time we humans have experienced climate change. We know from historical accounts that the earth's weather patterns have altered in the past, causing wide spread crop failures and famine. Famine is often followed by disease epidemics, which capitalize on poor resistance because of poor nutrition. (See Chapter 27, **More Resources**, ***On the Web***, "The Little Ice Age," for more information.) With possible epidemics in mind, high quality organic food becomes even more important.

In reaction to rising food prices, many families are now purchasing lower quality food to help make ends meet. In addition, more people are visiting food closets than ever before. The food found there is typically less than fresh, and often of poor nutritional quality. Downgrading family nutrition is dangerous at a time when the human population is high, people are crowded into cities, and possible pandemics are already a concern.

Those profiteering on food don't care what you get to eat, or even if you end up going hungry. They are only concerned with their profit margin. Don't let corporate interests or profiteers determine whether or not you can provide your family with decent meals and continued good nutrition. Home gardens are amazing. We will explore gardening in Chapter 5, **Food Security 101** and Chapter 19, **Food Security and the Garden**. Near the end of the book, in Chapter 27, **More Resources** you will find a subsection on ***Gardening*** in the ***On the Web*** section. There is another section covering ***Sources for Gardeners***. You will also want to check out the ***Educational Opportunities*** section, also in Chapter 27; many of the organizations listed offer classes for those who learn best in hands-on workshop settings.

My grandmother was very interested in what are sometimes called "primitive skills." In addition to wild foods, medicinal plants, and gardening—she dug and processed clay, hand built containers, and pit fired her wares. She also collected natural materials for weaving baskets; cooked over fire and with hot rocks, among other skills. Gram stored all kinds of things in her attic and around the house: food and herbal medicine; string, rope, and twine; garden seeds and tools; extra clothes, and other necessary items. She said these things would help us survive, for awhile, when the Green World returned. Eventually, she said, we would need to produce these things on our own.

We can borrow on my grandmother's ideas (and other things learned along the way) to prepare ourselves for whatever the transition and the return to the Green World brings in the times ahead.

3. The Times Ahead

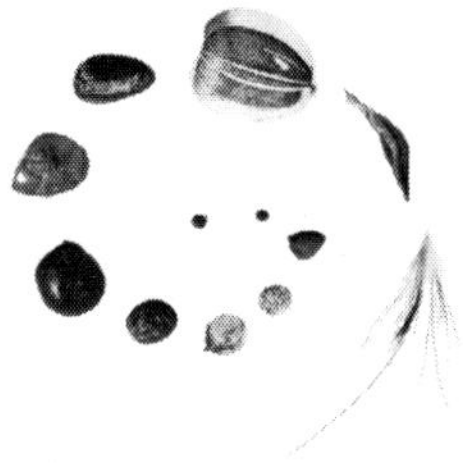

No matter what your politics, lifestyle, or religion, you have probably heard that we are in for a rough ride in the times ahead. If your eye is on the financial world, chances are you are very concerned about the deficit and the economy. Industrialists have related worries, the supplies of fossil fuels, minerals, and metal ores are being rapidly depleted. Ecologists are alarmed about the state of planet, our ecosystems, and food chains. Historians, who have studied the fall of previous civilizations, add their warnings to the news. Many religious people are focused on prophecy that tells of the end times, destruction of the planet, and a new beginning. Read the news any day and you will find reports of fires, floods, tornados, hurricanes, cyclones, and drought; along with the human suffering that accompanies these and other disasters.

Climate change is real. Whether you think it's part of a natural cycle, from all the carbon in the atmosphere, Mother Nature's revenge, or the Creator's wrath—something is definitely going on. Catastrophic weather destroys crops, as well as lives and homes. Crops are also disrupted by more subtle weather changes.

When it is hotter, cooler, or damper than usual—plant diseases and pests can run rampant, especially in large stands of single plants. Modern agriculture seems to be designed with pests and diseases in mind, with its large scale fields of single crops, which are as genetically identical as possible. While, this does make mechanical planting and harvesting feasible; it also provides the perfect setting for pests and diseases to flourish. Climate change has already helped tip the balance in favor of pests and diseases in some areas of the world. Our own agricultural areas may soon follow.

Many of us, especially those that lived through the sixties and seventies, are well aware that modern life was never built on sustainable principals. However, the majority of people in power are still more concerned about dollars and cents than with caring for our ecosystems. This unsustainable system is faltering. The world's food reserves are at an all time low, the population is at an all time high, and the agricultural outlook is alarming.

Individuals, families, and small communities need to get serious about food security and sustainability. For those who don't prepare, the times ahead may be very hungry. In fact, in parts of the world, the hungry times have already begun. We need the kind of food sustainability that not only provides for our families, but that flows outwards to our communities, regions, and the planet. This food security will last, not only through our lifetimes, but continue on to the generations that follow. This might seem like a tall order. But the research has already been done. We all have ancestors that, at one time, lived in harmony with the land. We can bring back the old wisdom and weave it into our lives again. As you read through this book, you will find the path back to that wisdom.

Meanwhile, it is important to know, to remember, why we are here; to fall back on spiritual beliefs, to call up memories of our elders' and ancestors' teachings. While we busy ourselves with the work of keeping our bodies nourished, our memories and beliefs will nourish the deeper work, which will help us build the sustainability we truly need.

4. Sustainability

Sustainability might seem an odd concept, if you haven't already been educating yourself on ecology and organics. To best understand what is meant by this term, it may help to take a look at what is not sustainable. Modern Western culture has encouraged us to use non-renewable resources and pollution causing chemicals for nearly all our needs. This really cannot go on for the long term, because the resources are getting used up and we are being inundated with toxic chemicals. So we say that modern Western culture is unsustainable. It produces environmental degradation that contributes to ill health and the collapse of the ecosystems we depend on.

Anything that is truly sustainable, on the other hand, can go on indefinitely. For instance, sustainable organic gardening uses techniques that do not cause soil erosion, pollution, or other environmental degradation. Through the use of compost and mulch, it becomes a self renewing practice—you don't need to use polluting or non-renewable fertilizers. Encouraging diversity in the garden lessens the impact of pests, which eliminates the need to use toxic pesticides. Sustainable organic gardening does not wear out the soil. The same plot of land can be gardened or farmed as long as we have descendants who care to nurture the land.

You will find I use the word "sustainable" a lot in this book. I use it to identify processes, ideas, skills, and foods that will not cause the ecosystems that support us to collapse. I am also, often, implying something more. For me, something that is sustainable is not only environmentally friendly; it is something that will outlast modern civilization's dependence on nonrenewable resources.

My grandmother taught me to think in terms of the time when the cement and asphalt world would disappear. She steeped me in this deep understanding of sustainability without ever uttering the word. Gram is certainly not the only person who has followed this path in her thinking. Researcher, Jason Godesky, has a large body of well documented writing on these topics. He has studied the historical collapse of cultures and civilizations, and his conclusions about where we are headed are very compelling. His research and writing point us towards the idea that we need to learn skills that will serve us beyond the fall of modern culture. (You will find the address to his web site in Chapter 27, **More Resources**, ***On the Web***.) Many of the skills that he and my grandmother would recommend learning are outlined in Chapter 22, Useful Skills.

Let's not waste any time. For many of us, our first concern is keeping our families fed. "Food Security" is another way to express the idea of food sustainability, and that is the subject of the next chapter.

5. Food Security 101

Many cultures that came before us knew it was wise to store a few years worth of food—as insurance against drought, pestilence, and other crop failures. These cultures we also involved in food production. Gardening, animal husbandry, gathering wild foods, fishing, and hunting, as well as drying and storing food—were on-going endeavors. We can learn from their examples and store food as insurance, while we get started producing at least some of our own supplies.

We will be looking at food storage in depth beginning in Chapter 7, **Storing Staples Securely**. In our initial food storage plans, many folks will be working with purchased supplies, primarily. Eventually we need to follow our ancestors lead and replenish our stores with local and home grown produce.

Sustainable organic agriculture and gardening are the true keys to food security. The more food we can grow in backyards, containers, on windowsills and roofs, in community gardens, and through community supported agriculture and small farms, the better off we are. The cost of food is based, in large part, on supply and demand. When we get involved with the supply end of food production, we not only improve our own food security—we relieve some of the demand, which will improve food security for those who are unable to grow any of their own.

Once you get comfortable with gardening, plan to grow more food than you need each year. Dry or otherwise store the surplus for winter, for variety through the seasons, and to help feed others who can't garden. Through a combination of storing and growing food, and then storing part of what you grow, you can take responsibility for your family's food security. Gardening will be covered in more depth in Chapter 19, **Food Security and the Garden**. You will also be interested in Chapter 20, **Old Time Food Preservation and Storage**; Chapter 22, **Useful Skills**; and the ***Sources for Gardeners*** section of Chapter 27, **More Resources**.

If you don't have the space to garden at home, the American Community Garden Association can help you find (or start) a community garden anywhere in the US or Canada. Check out their web site at: <http://www.communitygarden.org/>. (See the ***On the Web*** section of Chapter 27, **More Resources**, for tips on finding public access computers and instruction.)

Community Supported Agriculture is an alternative for anyone who doesn't feel ready or able to garden. Often referred to as "CSA's," these farms are supported financially and sometimes with the labor of their members. You purchase a share in the farm, which entitles you to a share in the farms production. Some farms ask for a small work commitment in addition to their share fee; others accept work exchanges for a portion of, or even the entire fee. There are CSA's that focus on vegetables, others that grow grain, and some that produce a combination of vegetables, dairy, eggs, and/or poultry. CSA's offer many opportunities for both urban and rural people to get involved with food production and food security. This web site will help you find a CSA near you: <http://www.umassvegetable.org/food_farming_systems/csa/resources.html>.

Many organic farms also accept volunteers; in exchange for training, for produce, and sometimes for room and board. Some farms accept short term commitments; others only accept those able to volunteer for full months or seasons. Volunteering on a small farm can be part (or all) of your food security plan. To learn more and find farms both near and far that accept volunteers visit: <http://www.wwoof.org/howworks.asp>. They have information on volunteer opportunities on organic farms, world-wide.

Gardening, whether at home or in a community garden, joining a CSA, volunteering or patronizing a small local organic farm—will help you provide a sustainable, long term, food security plan for your family.

Before we look at food storage and gardening in more depth, let's think about location. Where we live makes a huge difference in our quality of life. As nonrenewable resources dwindle and the effects of climate change accelerate, our location will have a big impact on our efforts towards sustainability.

6. Location, Location, Location

Location is important to many of life's ventures; however, most of us have never thought about it in regards to food security. With growing demands on the world's food production and dwindling reserves caused by climate change, crop failures, ethanol production, and the encroachment of industry and urbanization on agricultural land—location in regards to food security is something many of us should think about.

Those now living in large cities, at low elevation, in a floodplain, where the growing season is short, within 100 miles of the ocean or other large body of water, near melting glaciers, or in desert regions—need to think about how sustainable their location really is. The combined realities of climate change and declining oil production need to be taken into account. We need to know that our surrounding countryside and can produce all the food and water necessary for the people living nearby. And we need to determine if the countryside near where we live will become inundated as oceans rise or turn into a desert as water sources dry up, among other things.

Finding the necessary information to evaluate your location will take a little research. A good starting topic is the source of water used for irrigation and drinking. Water is often supplied by lakes or rivers, springs, wells, or glacial melt. To find your local source, use the Internet to search the name of your region, the word "irrigation," a backslash, and then "water sources." Here is an example I tried: Sacramento Valley irrigation / water sources. Lots of information on water sources, as well as information on agricultural pollution came up.

Once you know the local source of water, both for irrigation and drinking, you will want to know the future outlook. If the articles that came up in the first search don't address future supplies, search on: irrigation outlook / Sacramento River, for instance. You might also want to search on the drought incidence for your area. Another useful search, water shed / your region, will produce many interesting and informative articles.

If your region's water is primarily from wells, you may need to do a little more sleuthing. Wells are supplied by aquifers, which are underground lakes or rivers that saturate and slowly move through deep layers of rock or soil. Most aquifers are being depleted much faster than nature can restore them. This situation is not sustainable. When you search on a region's water source, the names of any aquifers will come up in the results. You can then do a search on the aquifer to find out if it is declining.

Folks who live near melting glaciers should consider that surface water levels may temporarily rise, only to subside as the glacier disappears. Projections are available on the Internet for most areas. Use a map to find out the names of local glaciers; then search for projections. Glaciers are often a regions' only reliable source of water. Find out about other water sources, and how long it is projected to take the glaciers to melt. Yes, I know, this is all a lot to think about, but it is better to start now and be prepared.

If you find that water resources are declining, you might explore water catchment systems. If you live in an area where you get plenty of rain, and you have room to for a large cistern or two, you just may be able to catch all the water you need. Chapter 21, **Gram, the Green World, Oxygen**

& Water, has a section on ***Water Development On-Line*** where you will find a web site address that has links to a world of information on water catchment.

Those in low rainfall areas may find that catchment is not feasible. If this is the case, it may be time to consider relocating. You can read about one family that made this decision in *Animal, Vegetable, Miracle.* For more information see the ***Recommended Reading*** section of Chapter 27, **More Resources**. After you assess your water situation, it is time to look at regional food sustainability and its connection to petroleum and fuel.

As petroleum reserves dwindle and fuel becomes more expensive, locally grown food will be the best buy. Internet searches can help you determine if your region produces the food you need. Start with the name of your region, a backslash, and then dairy farms, egg production, etc. Follow through with whatever you normally eat, in separate searches. If, for instance, no grain is grown in the area, it will likely become more expensive or in shorter supply than in the regions that do produce grain. As you explore the information you find, you will have a lot of thinking to do.

For those living within 100 miles of the coast, especially if you are at a low elevation, raising sea levels and the increasing threats of tsunamis and tropical storms are very real considerations. You can use the Internet to explore these threats. Search on your area with a backslash and the words "projected sea level." Also try tsunamis, tropical storms, and anything else that may concern you. Here is an example of a possible search: Klamath California / tsunami danger.

As far as sustainability goes, most cities get low scores. Your personal food security is directly related to your community's food security. Even when you do your part, your neighbors may not. I once lived on the edge of what was called a "pocket ghetto" in the Sacramento area. Until I got a dog and a lock for my gate, I never got a ripe tomato. Had my neighbors been truly suffering, they would have found a way around the dog and the lock. The more people there are in any given area, the more pressure there will be on the available resources. This might incline you to explore moving to a more rural area.

Many find they have to take lower paying jobs to relocate to the country side. That is a personal decision that some people are not prepared to make. If you simply cannot leave an urban area, try to educate others in your neighborhood about food security. Take a gentle approach. If what you have to say sounds scary, others will simply tune you out. You might try focusing on planting trees that produce food. Imagine a different fruit or nut tree growing in every yard along your street or around the block. What an abundance you will all have to share beginning in just a few years.

If, on the other hand, you decide it is time to relocate, there is still much to think about. Some places on the planet are experiencing more frequent droughts or flooding. Many areas are becoming hotter; while a few are actually becoming cooler. Use the Internet to search on the regions that appeal to you. The topics you used to research your current area, for water and food sustainability, are good starting places.

Climate change, drought, earthquakes, fire danger, and flooding are a few other things you will want to explore for each region you are interested in. Keep in mind, there is no place on the planet that is perfectly safe, but some places are definitely safer than others. Before any move, make sure that you are not jumping from the frying pan into the fire. Learn as much as possible about any potential threats, and make decisions accordingly. Don't forget to look into everyday things, like schools, taxes, cost of living, and available jobs. Plenty of clean water and affordable housing are essential considerations.

The mere idea of moving is whelming for many. However, our efforts could be wasted by living in locations that don't support sustainability.

Once you have your location questions explored, it's time to take a look at forming a family food security plan. The first step is learning to store food securely, which is the subject of our next chapter.

7. Storing Staples Securely

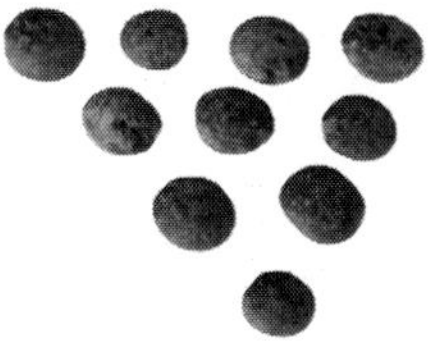

Once you're settled, or are simply set to make the best of where you are, you can begin to put together a food security plan. You will need some provisions for storing dry goods in a way that keeps them from spoiling, getting rancid or stale, infested with insects, raided by rodents, or ruined by other possible hazards. By the time you read through this chapter, you will know how to keep your food secure. (The following three chapters will help you choose the best foods to store to keep your family happy and healthy.)

The best food security plans include at least two strategies for food storage. The first strategy will cover long term (1 – 2 years) storage of staples, as insurance against crop failures and fluctuating prices. Long term storage is covered in detail in Chapter 17, **Your Food Storage Plan**. Emergency caches are the other strategy(s). They are used as insurance for natural disasters and other events that disrupt normal life. More information on emergency caches will be covered in Chapter 18, **Packing the Emergency Cache**. The rest of this chapter, and the chapters in between, will provide the information you need to complete your food storage plan and pack your emergency cache(s).

The following sections cover what you need to know to store staples securely, both for emergencies and for the long term.

Shelf Life:

The very first thing we need to consider is the shelf life of any food we may want to store. No matter what kind of food you buy or grow, it will only last so long. Ask the supplier how to read the codes on packages or labels. If there are no codes, ask about the average shelf life for each product or type of dry goods. In some cases you may have to contact the packager or manufacturer to get the information you need. Even commercial disaster meals have an expiration date. Plan on eating all stored food before it expires, by cycling it out of caches and long term storage and into the kitchen, on a regular basis.

There is no point in spending a pile of money on food that gets wasted, simply because it was stored past its useful life. Keep a notebook in the pantry with a list of what is on hand, how much, and when it will expire. At the front of the notebook list all of the stored items, with each entry followed by a page number. If you have food stored in more than one spot, note each item's location. Then give each item a full page of its own. That way you can keep track of supplies. You'll know what needs used soon and what needs replaced.

If you purchase or store more than you can use, donate any unneeded food still sealed in the original packages to a local food closet, at least two or three months before they expire. Expired food, which has not spoiled, can also be fed to pets or livestock. Other unused and unusable food can be fed to red worms or the compost heap. (*The Complete Compost Gardening Guide* has all you need to know about red worms and compost heaps. See the listing under ***Recommended Reading*** in Chapter 27, **More Resources**.) The best plan, however, is to only store what you will use, so you don't waste your hard earned money. Chapter 17, **Your Food Storage Plan** will help you determine how much of what sorts of food you should store. Meanwhile, you will find more considerations that affect your food storage plan, starting on the next page.

Insects, Rodents, & Bears:

Insects: Many foods, especially bulk foods, are already infested with bug eggs when you purchase them. Freezing will kill most bug eggs. It is a good idea to put dry goods in the freezer for at least six hours; two full days is even more effective. (This is not necessary for processed foods sealed in jars or cans.) If your freezer forms frost, use flexible plastic, air and moisture proof containers and lids.

Ridged containers, such as glass jars can be used in frost free freezers. To allow for contraction and expansion during their stay in the freezer, loosen the lids a tiny bit; but remember to tighten them back up as soon as you take them out of the freezer. Read through the rest of this chapter before freezing dry goods. They will need proper care immediately after coming out of the freezer, so they do not become reinfested.

Choose containers carefully to safeguard food. Thick walled containers with thick air tight lids are essential to keep insects out. Any tiny space between the container and lid can allow insects to enter. Insects can also chew through paper, cardboard, and thin plastic. Don't head out to buy containers yet, there is more to think about than bugs when choosing containers, as you will see.

And, when it comes to bugs, there is more to think about than containers and freezing. To ensure bulk dry goods are not reinfested by frost hardy eggs or tiny breaches between container and lid, food grade diatomaceous earth is a good investment. It's available on-line and at larger natural food markets. One-quarter teaspoon of this dust, formed from the fossilized shells of diatoms, will protect a gallon container of dry goods. Simply sprinkle in a tiny bit, every so often, as you fill the container. (You can rinse it off before you cook the food; however, it won't hurt a bit if you simply eat it.) Adding a few dry bay leaves and dry hot peppers to the top of the container helps deter insects that find their food through the sense of smell. See the section on ***Sealing Your Containers***, at the end of this chapter, to make sure bugs don't get into the jars.

For the last word on bugs, here is a conversation I had with my grandmother, back in the day when I was a snub nosed kid.

Gram: "People from many different cultures around the world have eaten bugs from the beginning of time."
Me: "Let's just send them these, then."
Gram: "They won't hurt you, they are full of protein, and there are people starving for lack of protein right now."
Me: "Then let's send them these bugs, OK Gram?"
Gram: "Nobody ever died from eating a few bugs."
Me: "So?"
Gram: "Just eat them, they're good for you."
Me: "No! Yuck!"

Eating a few bugs probably won't hurt you, but if you are like me, well, you would just rather not. So, be careful how you store your food. On the other hand, someday, if our stores of diatomaceous earth run out or the electricity fails, we may have to take my Gram's advice and eat a few bugs.

Rodents: Never underestimate a rodent's ability to chew through thick plastic. Hungry rats, weasels, marmots, raccoons, and other animals do not find plastic containers or lids a deterrent of any kind. Food stored in plastic containers is safest when placed in rodent proof metal trash cans or storage lockers. Place these metal containers in a cool spot, out of the sun and away from sources of heat, so that the containers inside do not overheat and burst.

Bears: Your neighbors may have the best information on bear proofing emergency caches; because, hopefully, they have already learned to outsmart the local marauders. Ask them how to keep bears out of the trash and fruit trees and you will have the beginnings of a plan. For extra protection see ***Sealing Your Containers***, at the end of this chapter. Bears find food with their nose, air proof containers that have the addition of bay leaves and hot peppers can help keep them out of caches. Local native aromatics, such as dry pine needles or cedar sprigs, might work even better. Bears are very smart, and some may have learned to associate the scent of bay and hot peppers with food. Also, avoid sealing jars with bee wax in bear country. That is a scent they know and love.

You can look on-line or in backpacking and survivalist type books for information on bear proofing food caches. Before you purchase any "bear proof" receptacles, look for user reviews. To find reviews on-line: type in the product name with a backslash and the word "review." Here is an example: Bear Away Receptacles / reviews. Bears are a challenge; whatever you do, start with a small cache, so you won't be devastated if they outsmart you.

Potential Hazards Effect How Food is Stored:

Earthquakes, Hurricanes, & Tornadoes: Where these events are a potential problem, you have to think about the possibility of structure failure, trees falling, and possible landslides. A good strategy is to bury a cache of emergency food in shatter proof containers, enclosed in a rodent proof metal trash can or similar container. Choose a site that won't get buried under mud slides, inundated with water, or covered with falling debris. One to several small to medium sized metal trash-can(s) or extra large soup kettles should work well, depending on the size of your family. You want each hole to be one-half to three-quarters as deep as the receptacle or kettle. Line the hole with a large plastic garbage bag, to keep out moisture, and place the can or pot inside the bag. Wrap appropriately packaged food containers in newspaper or clean rags as a cushion, and place them in the can or other receptacle. If a source of sand is available, you can use it to fill the spaces between the containers for further insulation. The sand will also help keep rodents, spiders, and insects out of the cache. Cover the container securely, seal with duct tape or strips of wax soaked cloth (see ***Sealing Your Containers***, at the end of this chapter). Secure the garbage bag over the top of the can, to help keep soil moisture from seeping into the cache. A second bag placed over the top and tucked down the sides is a good idea. Then you can pile the loose dirt from the hole back over the top. Add a piece of statuary or a decorative rock to the top of the mound to mark the spot. This little exercise is a bit of work, but it may save your family from going hungry in an emergency. You will need to rotate the food out of this cache well before it expires, so don't forget to keep track of expiration dates.

High Rainfall or Humidity: Moisture is the enemy of stored food. In areas of high rainfall or humidity, extra steps are necessary to ensure grains, beans, and other dry goods don't absorb water and mold or mildew. Frost-free freezers, when working properly, are efficient at removing moisture. Freeze dry goods in their storage containers (with the lids off) overnight. Cover them tightly as soon as you take them out of the freezer. (If you get condensation inside the jars, and there is no frost in the freezer, the food is still moist and needs to spend more time in the freezer, with the lids off. Condensation outside the jars is normal and will not harm the food.) If you don't have access to a frost free freezer, packages of desiccant are a good investment. Most desiccants are reusable, follow package directions to refresh as needed. (Desiccant packets are sold through many bulk good outlets. You can also search for them on-line.) Food sent on a short trip through a food dehydrator, directly before being sealed in containers is a third option. No matter how you deal with humidity, you will definitely need air tight lids, see ***Sealing Your Containers***, at the end of this chapter.

Flooding: People have lived in areas prone to flooding since the beginning of time, and they are likely to continue to do so. Periodic flooding can actually improve crop land. Pest are often drowned or washed away, nutrients are replenished by silt, and aquifers are recharged. Flooding, as you already know, is catastrophic to home, life, livelihood, and livestock. Food containers should be water and air tight, shatterproof, and stored in a secure spot on high ground or in an attic. Don't forget to take bears, rodents, and other possible threats into consideration. Use care where you place the flood cache, you don't want it to become a falling hazard during a hurricane, tornado, or earthquake.

Fire: The buried cache suggested for Earthquakes, Hurricanes, & Tornadoes will work well for fires. Glass containers with metal lids are ideal. Look for lids that don't have plastic linings. These linings can vent toxins into food, if they get hot enough. Check around the house and second hand stores for old mayonnaise and other lids, that lack plastic linings. You may also be able to find a source of flat metal or glass disks that will work with canning jar rings. Seal these makeshift lids with strips of 100% cotton cloth dipped in bees wax. (See instructions in ***Sealing Your Containers***, at the end of this chapter.) Filling the space between the jars inside the cache with sand will provide non-toxic and non-flammable insulation.

Other Considerations:

Heat & Light reduce shelf life and destroy nutrients in foods. For food stored in the house, choose a dark, dry, cool pantry or closet against an inside wall. Dry basements and root cellars are other good spots. When food must be stored where it will be exposed to heat and light, many common household materials can be used for insulation. Old pillows, blankets, and other fabric; newspaper; and recycled packing material are possibilities. As these items are flammable, keep them away from sources of flame or spark. Rodents and birds would love to rob the insulation for nesting material, so keep this in mind when making a plan.

An old refrigerator or freezer that still has its insulation, kept indoors or in the shade, is a perfect receptacle for rodent and bug proof containers. (Lock it up, so a child doesn't climb in and become trapped.) Other metal containers that you can insulate and secure, indoors or in a shady area, can also be used.

Rancidity: Food becomes rancid, primarily, by exposure to temperature changes in the presence of oxygen. Containers for storing dry goods should be filled as close to the top as practical, to reduce air space and oxygen. When you are repackaging bulk items it is a good idea to have gallon, half gallon, and quart sized containers on hand. That way when get near the bottom of a twenty-five pound bag of rice, for instance, you are not left with a small amount of grain to be stored in a large container with lots of air space at the top. If you do end up with a half full container, keep that one aside for immediate use. Closets in cool rooms with food stored along inside walls are good choices for temperature stability. For other ideas see: ***Earthquakes, Hurricanes, & Tornadoes*** for information on a buried cache; and ***Heat & Ligh***t, for insulation ideas. Both of these sections are found in this chapter.

Physical Hazards: Food containers can pose hazards during earthquakes, floods, tornadoes, and hurricanes. Keep large or heavy items in a low secure spot, where they won't hinder escape routes should they fall, roll, or slide. Many utility companies have free pamphlets detailing emergency preparedness. They will give you ideas on securing storage areas. The pamphlets are usually free, on request. Also check the phone book for tips, and with the library or book store for titles on emergency preparedness. You should find hints on securing shelves and the items stored on the shelves. Be informed, prepared, and safe.

Ethics: There is a huge difference between storing a year or two's worth of food that will actually be eaten, and hoarding food out of fear—or in hopes of profit. When rice shortages first surfaced, prices climbed quickly. Rice soon became subject to rationing in some areas, and a matter of waiting in line in others. All sense seemed to fly out the window; folks who don't often eat rice got in line to purchase as many 25 pound bags as the limit allowed. Some of them did this repeatedly, creating more demand and causing prices to rise even higher. This panic shopping made rice much more expensive, and less available, for those who depend on it the most.

There are people around the world who cannot afford a decent diet. Malnutrition and starvation are on the rise. You can help by only purchasing what you really need and taking proper care of these purchases to guard against spoilage and waste. This way, we are not contributing excess demand on limited food resources. The more demand those of us in developed countries place on the world's food supplies, the less food is available to those with the highest risk for malnutrition and starvation. Keep track of expiration dates, and donate any excess food to a local food closet—well before the expiration dates are reached. By law, expired food cannot be distributed, even when it might save lives.

Space, Containers, & Labeling:

Storage Space: Food will last the longest when it is stored in a cool, dry place. Before you purchase supplies, keep in mind how much storage space you have. Being prepared should not mean that one's quality of life is impaired by boxes and canisters cluttering up living and working space.

Storage Containers need to be rodent, moisture, air, and insect proof, as well as scrupulously clean and dry. If you purchase bulk food in 25 – 50 pound sacks, repackage it into smaller sized containers. The sacks are not insect or rodent proof and they won't prevent food from becoming stale or rancid. If you are subject to earthquakes, hurricanes, or tornados, shatter proof containers are a good idea. On the other hand, when fires are the main threat, choose glass or metal containers with metal lids.

A selection of gallon, quart, and pint containers will serve you well. Be sure to read all of this chapter, and the previous chapter, **Location, Location, Location**, before purchasing any containers. The specific hazards your food may be subjected to need to be taken into account. Once you are ready to look for containers, check with second hand stores, recycling centers, and ask at any restaurant or deli that you frequent. Used gallon, half gallon, and other sized jars can usually be found, inexpensively. Also check with bulk food distributors, farm and feed stores, larger grocery stores, second hand shops, and recycle centers.

Labeling: First freeze filled containers (to kill bug eggs, see section on ***Insects***, in this chapter) and then let them return to room temperature. Then label containers with the contents, the date purchased, the expiration date, the source, and attach any labels from items you have repackaged. You can use a wide roll of clear packaging tape, and completely cover the labels as you attach them to the jars. It's a good idea to put a second label inside the jar, before sealing it, in case the one outside is damaged or lost. This will help you keep track of food that hasn't expired, and what needs to be eaten first. If any spoils before its expiration, you may be able to contact the company for refunds.

Sealing Your Containers: After containers of food have been frozen (which kills most insects and their eggs) allow them to return to room temperature. Reinforce the lids with duct tape, or alternatively—if you are using glass jars with metal lids, with strips of cloth dipped in melted wax. (Most tape and wax becomes brittle and ineffective in freezing temperatures. For food that may be subjected to freezing temps during storage, you might want to use bees wax—which holds up to freezing a little better. When the weather begins to thaw, check the integrity of the seals.) For the wax and cloth technique, melt the wax over low heat—in a double boiler or an old electric frying pan. If it begins smoking even faintly, remove from heat immediately (and carefully) to avoid starting a fire. Use a pair of old gloves to dip the cloth strips in the wax. Leave a small strip at one end of the cloth wax free, to help unseal the jar when you are ready to use it. Avoid dripping hot wax onto skin and other fragile surfaces. Smooth strips over the junction of lids and jars and allow them to cool. The jars are now ready to store, just be sure to label them first.

Next we will take a look at the types of food that work well for storage.

8. Wise Food Choices for Storage

There are many choices to make when planning storage for food security. Purchasing pricey pre-packaged dehydrated emergency meals may seem convenient, but food that isn't happily eaten before it expires becomes a huge waste. Here are some less expensive suggestions that you can use to start a food storage plan. As you read them over, keep in mind what you and your family normally like to eat. Each food item, beginning below and continuing on the following pages, is designated as appropriate for long term storage or for emergency use. Determining the amount and mix of foods to store will be covered in Chapter 17, **Your Food Storage Plan**.

Canned Goods: Storing at least a little canned tuna, chicken, salmon, or other meats in emergency caches—will provide some extra protein during difficult times. These foods make great sandwich fillings, so when you need to cycle them out of your caches you can plan a picnic. Other canned goods are worth storing, for families that normally use them. To avoid bursting, don't store food sealed in cans and jars in high, freezing, or widely fluctuating temperatures. Metal cans or jars with metal lids should not be exposed to overly moist or humid conditions for long periods of time, because of the possibility of rust. A non-electric can opener must be stored with any caches that contain canned goods. {Long Term & Emergency}

Packaged Snacks: Single servings of crackers, cookies, nuts, dried fruit, and beef jerky make good additions to emergency caches. When the power is out, the house is damaged or worse—having some high energy, nutritious food, that needs no preparation, will help you get by the first few days. Single serving packets make eating and rationing easy; however, check the expiration dates. These items can have short shelf lives. When it is time to rotate them, they can become party favors, Halloween goodies, Christmas stocking and Easter Basket stuffers, or simply snacks. {Emergency}

Pasta: Pasta is light weight, carbohydrate dense, and easy to prepare; which makes it a good emergency food. Most pasta has a fairly long shelf life. Spaghetti and other similar flat varieties will help conserve space. Note expiration dates, purchase no more than will be eaten before it expires, and include an appropriate cooking pot and strainer in any emergency caches. Plan an Italian themed dinner every so often, to use up the pasta as it is cycled into the kitchen. {Long Term & Emergency}

Powdered Milk and Eggs: Most people would agree, these products do not compare to their fresh counterparts. Before purchasing them for emergency purposes, think about how you will use them as they need to be rotated out of your caches. (Don't forget to check the expiration dates.) Powdered eggs make decent omelets and the eggs and milk can be used in baked goods, puddings, and quiches. <Emergency>

Nuts: Nutrient and energy dense, many nuts make good choices for food storage. Unfortunately, they are expensive and high in fat, which can lead to rancidity—unless they are carefully stored. Nuts store best raw, in their own shells, where they can stay fresh for up to a year or longer. Shelled nuts take up much less space, but they won't stay fresh nearly as long. Store them in a cool, dry spot that is not subject to bright light or wide temperature changes. They also need protection from insects and rodents, see Chapter 7, **Storing Staples Securely** for more information. {Long Term & Emergency}

Water: Everyone needs to have an emergency water plan. Having some bleach on hand, as well as water filters—is a very good idea. A large kettle that you can use to boil water is a necessity. You can also store bottled drinking water under a bed or in another location that will stay dark and cool. Bottled water has an expiration date, so log it in your notebook (see ***Shelf Life***, Chapter 7, **Storing Staples Securely**). You can store tap water for up to six months, in clean, sterile, food safe containers. If the water clouds or turns green, boil and filter it before using. Store water in a different location than dry goods, leaking bottles can ruin food. Here is a great web site with emergency water information: <http://www.wawater.com/emergency/>. You might want to print out the page and keep it with your emergency caches. {Emergency}

Whole Grains and Dry Beans: Even though prices have been going up, these foods are still the best buy for your food storage dollar. They store for two years (or longer), they are nutrient dense, easy to prepare, and as an added bonus—they can be planted to produce more food. If you are not in the habit of eating whole grains and beans, maybe it's time to pick up a cookbook or two and begin experimenting. See the **Recommended Reading** section of Chapter 27, **More Resources**, several good cookbooks are listed. {Long term & Emergency}

9. Poor Choices for Food Storage

The worst food choices are low in nutritional value and high in moisture or air. Additionally anything that needs refrigeration or freezing should not be considered part of a food security plan. When natural disasters strike electricity often fails. Below, and on the following pages, you will find a list of some poor choices for food storage. Please keep in mind that some items that are inappropriate for long term storage are fine for emergency caches, as long as they are rotated frequently.

Low nutritional value foods have no place in a food security plan. Natural disasters can spread contagions; especially when wells are inundated or sewer lines break. We need to keep our nutrition up to keep our resistance up. These low nutrition foods should not be included: popcorn, chips, most crackers—unless whole grain, rice cakes, candy, pastries, flavored drinks, and any other empty calorie snacks, deserts, or packaged food items.

Foods with high moisture content are subject to rapid spoilage and they can hasten the demise of other foods in the cache or long term storage, by raising humidity or leaking. Here are some examples of foods to avoid: syrup, butter, cakes and cookies, bread, fresh fruit and veggies, potatoes, onions, and anything else likely to mold or rot.

Crushable foods are not among the best choices either. Most crushable foods are also found in other sections in this chapter. They are usually low in nutrition, contain lots of air, and are high priced when you look at the cost per serving. Most cereals would fall in this category, as well as puffed grain products, crackers, many snacks, and chips.

Food packaged in cardboard containers make poor choices for a number of reasons. Most of the cost of these items is for packaging and processing, making them a poor buy. Many of these foods have poor nutritional value, are easily crushed, contain a lot of air space in the package or product—causing them to take up precious space and making them prone to rancidity. They can come from the market already contaminated with bug eggs—which is hard to manage in prepackaged food. Some examples are: cereal, crackers and cracker crumbs, cake mixes, flavored rice and pasta, etc. However, for short term emergency caches, some of these items can be useful. If you choose to use these foods, don't forget to rotate them before they expire.

Refrigerated or frozen foods: Any sort of natural disaster is likely to cause at least a temporary break in electrical service. Climate change is already threatening our electrical service. Droughts take their toll on hydro-power and on nuclear energy production. The latter requires vast amounts of water for cooling. Some nuclear power plants have been close to shutting down when water levels have fallen because of drought. Nuclear power is only cost effective when the plants run continuously. Earthquakes also seem to be more frequent. They can destabilize hydro and nuclear energy production. The price of electricity is also tied to the price of fuel. Most of the electricity in the United States is generated by burning fossil fuel, in one form or another. We have already experienced rapidly fluctuating fuel prices; the price of electricity is sure to follow suit. Canned and dried food is a much safer bet.

Flour and baking mixes aren't suitable for long term storage for a number of reasons. They go rancid easily and loose nutritional value quickly. When they get wet, they are ruined, unlike whole grains and dry beans; which can be dried out completely, stored, and used, when they haven't been wet for long. When flour or baking mix becomes infested with bugs, it is pretty hard to pick the bugs out, and the bug feces are in the mix to stay. If bugs get into dry grain or beans you can pick out the ruined bits, shake or wash the rest, and dry them out completely. (The section on ***Insects*** in Chapter 7, **Storing Staples Securely**, will help you keep grains and beans bug free.) For those who can't live without flour, look for a hand operated mill or grinder. No other flour will compare in flavor or nutritional value.

Now that you have a good idea on the types of foods that make wise and poor choices for storage, it is time to think about a nutritional balanced diet, which is the subject of the next chapter, **Balance is Everything**.

10. Balance is Everything

When planning for long term food storage and for emergency caches, you must keep nutritional balance in mind. You will need plenty of complex carbohydrates to fuel muscle and brain cells. Protein is necessary for proper immune system function and for healing and repair. Anti-oxidants, phyto-nutrients, vitamins, and minerals can help ward off disease and improve feelings of well being. A little healthy fat is good for keeping our physical energy at optimum levels and for the integrity of cell walls. Calcium is important to keep bones and teeth strong, and it also helps the immune system and the nerves. Last but not least, dietary fiber will help keep elimination processes running smoothly. Sources of each of these nutrients are outlined, below and on the following pages, as storage and garden options.

Complex Carbohydrates: The best sources of complex carbohydrates, for long term storage, are whole grains and beans. Whole grain pasta, hot cereal, and crackers are good choices for emergency caches, because they quick and easy to prepare. For sustainability, dry beans can be grown in a home garden. If you have room, you can also experiment with growing a number of kinds of grain. See Chapter 27, **More Resources** for information on the seed company, Bountiful Gardens, which is listed in the section, ***Sources for Gardeners***. They offer small lots of grain and bean seed for home gardeners.

Protein: Beans and grains supply plenty of protein when served together. However, in times of stress or heavy physical demands, or in the case of growing children, some supplemental protein is in order. Canned fish, chicken, or other meats make a good source of protein for inclusion in emergency caches. Raw nuts, especially when offered in variety, are superior protein sources. Soy beans are another option. Soy is available in a number of forms, including dry beans, textured vegetable protein, and protein powder. Soy beans and nut trees are easy to grow. For those near a stream, river, lake, or coast line—fishing is another option for providing an on-going source of protein.

Fat: We actually need small amounts of high quality fat in our diet for maximum health. Raw nuts offer superior sources of healthy fats, including a range of essential fatty acids. You can store raw nuts in their shells for at least a year. (Nuts that show signs of decay or mold, or that smell or taste stale or rancid should be composted.) For cooking oil, big box stores such as Sam's Club and Costco have good deals. Store oil separately from your dry goods; leaking oil can ruin other supplies. Besides kitchen use, you can use a little oil as a replacement for lotion and insect repellent. For information on producing fat sustainably, see Chapter 11, **Process Your Own Fats and Oils**.

Dietary Fiber: Grains and beans supply plenty of fiber, as do veggies and fruit. When these foods are a significant part of the diet, you usually don't need to think about adding additional fiber. However, if regularity is a problem, look into natural remedies before they are needed. Flax, psyllium, prunes, and figs are good sources of soluble fiber. At least one of these ought to help, and they can all be grown in the garden. Be sure to drink plenty of water, it is also necessary for natural regularity.

Calcium how to get it, and how much you actually need is a subject of much controversy. The best information I have come across is in an out of print book titled, *CalciYum!* The introductory and concluding chapters and the appendix may reform your thinking on how much calcium is needed for health. The conclusions are well researched and sources of more information are given. *CalciYum!* is by David and Rachelle Bronfman, published by Bromedia, 1998. It is still available through Amazon.com and used book outlets at reasonable prices. (My local library was able to borrow it from another library, for a $1.00 fee.) Whatever side of the calcium arguments you lean toward, plan on having a source of calcium in the diet, for the long term and for emergencies.

I favor using ground oyster shell (sold as a chicken supplement) as a soil amendment, and eating lots of greens. Those oyster shells will continue to provide small amounts of calcium to my soil and garden for many years. Deep rooted veggies and edible wild plants are good sources of calcium. For more information on deep rooted vegetables, herbs, and wild plants, as well as plants known to accumulate calcium see *Designing and Maintaining Your Edible Landscape Naturally* (listed in the Recommended Reading section of Chapter 27, **More Resources**). You may also want calcium supplements for emergency caches. Calcium not only builds strong bones and teeth, it helps us deal with stress and it strengthens the immune system.

Anti-oxidants, Phyto-nutrients, Vitamins, and Minerals are necessary for health and well being. They also help keep our immune systems in good working order, which is covered in more detail in Chapter 13, **Don't Forget Your Immune System**. While these nutrients are best provided by a variety of fresh produce—you can make do with canned or dried foods temporarily, in emergency situations. Think greens, berries, and wild food for great nutrition. Dark, bright, and intensely colored foods, like beets and yams, are also nutritionally dense. Growing these foods in the garden, and learning about wild foods, will provide these important nutrients to your family.

Vitamin B12 is necessary for proper growth in children and it is helpful for everyone in stressful situations. Unfortunately, for vegetarians, it is not found in abundance in plant based foods. While some adults seem to do fine on inadequate amounts, the same cannot be said for children. Canned clams and oysters are good sources for emergency caches. A three ounce serving twice a week is all you need. Wild trout is also a good source, three ounces nearly meets the minimum daily requirement. If shellfish or trout aren't on the menu, consider a supplement, unless you have a source of game or pastured meat for canning and drying. Pastured or wild animals that have plenty of fresh air, sunshine, and exercise (and that don't live in their own excrement) produce the only animal products any of us should eat. See *In Defense of Food* and *You Can Farm*, listed in ***Recommended Reading***, Chapter 27, **More Resources.** For more information on Vitamin B12 see: <http://dietary-supplements.info.nih.gov/factsheets/vitaminb12.asp#h2>

Water, water, water: If yours comes out of a tap, you need an emergency plan. Drinking water can stored for at least six months. (Keep it away from dry goods, and take note of bottled water's expiration date—check the label or ask your grocer.) You will need a long term plan, such as water from a creek, river, well, or spring. Keep a kettle or soup pot large enough to boil a day's supply on hand. Plan to filter the water, after you boil it and it has returned to room temperature. (Water filters designed for backpackers can be purchased through sporting goods suppliers. Homemade water filters and more information on storage are covered in Chapter 21, **Gram, the Green World, Oxygen & Water.**) You will also need a separate container to store purified water in, so you can boil more before the first batch runs out. A camp stove with plenty of fuel is a possible emergency measure. (Hot pads, oven mitts, or hand towels are a must.) A set up made with rocks and a sturdy grate, where you can burn wood—ought to work when the weather is mild. Stock up on firewood if you have room and if it might be in short supply.

Now that we've got a balanced diet in the making, it's time to take a look at how to sustainably produce our own fat and oil, right at home.

11. Process Your Own Fats and Oils

Most of us purchase all the oils and fats we use. We may have forgotten, or perhaps we never knew, that there was a time when most folks produced all they needed right at home. Animal fat is easy to process. If you eat meat, you may already be discarding all the fat you need. Producing vegetable oil is a little more difficult, but it can also be accomplished at home.

Instructions on processing animal fat begin below, after which you will find instructions for vegetable oil.

Animal Fat: When rendered and clarified and then stored in air and moisture proof containers, animal fat will keep a surprisingly long time. If you already eat meat, or plan to raise animals for slaughter, you will have plenty of fat to render. Wild animals, depending on the season, also produce enough fat for rendering and clarifying. Rendering is the process of removing the fat from the animal tissues.

Home rendering is best accomplished by placing trimmed fat (in pieces no more than two inches thick) in a Dutch oven or deep roasting pan and slowly heating it in the oven, on the stove top, or over a slow fire. The exact temperature necessary will vary, depending on the season and the source of the fat. Keep a close watch, through the whole process, you don't want the fat to boil or smoke. After the first 30 minutes you should notice melting. If not, turn up the heat ever so slightly, and adjust as needed.

You will need another pot, or a wide mouthed heat proof container, to hold the fat as it liquefies. As the solid fat melts and begins to accumulate in the bottom of the pan, carefully dip it out. Be extra careful not to spill the hot fat or splatter it on anyone's skin. When most of the fat has melted, you may be left with some crispy, bubbly, husks. If you want to get as much oil out of the husks as possible, carefully crunch them up with a potato or bean masher, and continue to heat slowly. You will have to pour any remaining fat through a fine mesh heat resistant strainer. Once you have collected as much fat as you are going to get, it is time to clarify it.

Besides the fat you render, you can clarify pan drippings, bacon fat, and the fat that comes to the top of the kettle when you make broth or soup. You will need a pot that holds at least twice as much as the amount of fat you plan to clarify, a little vinegar, and at least half as much good clean water as you have fat. Place the fat in the pot, add a teaspoon of vinegar for each quart of fat (it doesn't need to be exact), and slowly pour in the water. The water level should be no closer than two and a half inches from the top of the pot. Slowly bring the fat and water to a boil over medium heat, stirring occasionally. Allow to boil for five minutes and then turn the heat off. (Keep an eye on it. Don't let the pot to boil over.) Once all movement stops, you can use a skewer, a spoon, the corner of a paper towel or of a clean piece of cotton fabric—to pick specks of foreign matter from the top of the fat. Once the surface is cleaned, let it sit undisturbed until cool.

Once the fat and water are cool, touch the top of the fat to see how solid it is. If it gives to the touch, move the pot to the coolest spot you can find, and let it continue to solidify. (The fridge works fine. For some types of fat a brief time in the freezer is even better.) When the fat is solid, use a knife to cut it into quarters and then pry a piece from the pot. Carefully scrap any foreign matter from the top and bottom of the fat, and repeat for the rest of the pieces. I generally repeat the boiling, stirring, cooling, and scraping until the fat is white and I no longer find any foreign matter. (The scrapings are edible, they just won't keep long.)

Before storing, any liquid left from the clarifying process needs to be released. Gently heat the fat in a clean dry container until just melted, and then lower the heat enough to keep the fat from cooking, while still remaining fluid. Hold it in this fluid state and stir frequently with a clean dry spoon, for at least 30 minutes, or until water vapor no longer rises from the surface. Then pour the fat into sterile, dry canning jars. If you are going to run the fat through a pressure canner, be sure to leave at least ¾ inch headroom. (Or follow the manufacturer's instructions.)

If you are not canning the fat, you can fill the jars to within ¼ inch of the top, to reduce oxygen inside the jars. Clarified fat will keep several months—as long as it is stored in clean, air and moisture proof containers, in a cool spot. (For longer storage pressure can it at 15 pounds for at least 45 minutes, or follow the manufactures guidelines.) Fat that discolors, molds, or develops an odor should be discarded.

Vegetable Oil: Depending on your climate, there are many different plants that can be grown to produce vegetable oil. Those who live in mild or sub-tropical areas have a choice of many oil bearing seeds and fruits, including olives, avocados, and jojoba beans. Growing hardy oil rich nuts—such as butternuts, walnuts, and almonds—is a possibility in cooler regions. Annual oil seeds, like the rape seed which is used to produce canola oil, thrive in cool summer areas and do well farther north.

The lowest tech way to obtain oil from plant material is to crush or pound the seeds, nuts, or fruits and then boil them in water. You may find that containing the plant matter in a muslin bag is helpful for producing cleaner oil. (You may also need to experiment with using under-ripe, ripe, and over-ripe produce; as well as fresh and dried plant material.)

While boiling, the oil will rise to the top of the pot, where it is skimmed off and strained. If you find that there is still a lot of organic matter in the oil, you may have to repeat the boiling process a few times. Use fresh water, stir vigorously, skim and strain during each repetition. Don't let your pot boil over, vegetable oil is flammable. Once the oil is clean and strained, pour it in to a tall glass or jar and let any remaining water separate out. Pour or dip off the separated oil. You may have to repeat this process a few times to be sure you have water free oil. You can remove more water from the oil by gently heating it at a low temperature, and holding it in this warm state for 30 minutes or so, stirring frequently. When water vapor no longer rises from the oil, you know it is safe to store.

Water free oil stores for several months, or even longer, if kept in air tight containers placed in a cool spot. Use the smallest container that will hold the oil, to reduce the incidence of rancidity. Oil that still contains some water needs used right away, it will spoil quickly. Oil and water mixes can be used in baked goods, in the bottom of roasting pans, for basting meats and poultry, as a base for salad dressings, or even as a skin moisturizer. However you use it, shake well to mix the oil and water and then proceed.

If you are interested in producing cold pressed oils or reading instruction for processing specific oil types, visit the "Household Cyclopedia" at: <http://www.publicbookshelf.com/public_html/The_Household_Cyclopedia_of_General_Information/>. Click on "Household Advice and Information," scroll down and click on "How to make oils." You will have to scroll down again to read the article.

Next we are going to take a look at how our shopping habits can contribute to food security, not only for us, but for everyone.

12. Shop Flexible, Shop Wise

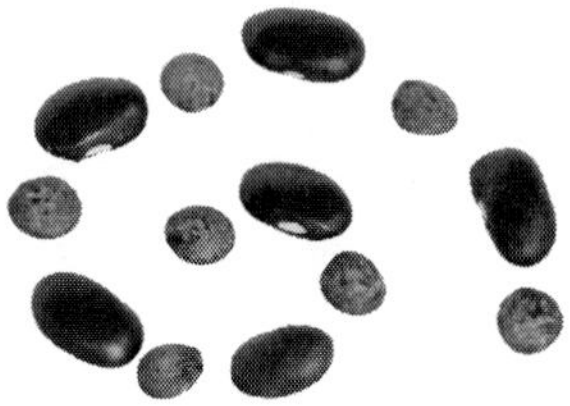

Flexibility is an important aspect of food security. Many of us primarily eat what we enjoyed eating as children. This is not to say that we don't have more adult tastes and that we don't make better choices. However, think about how long it has been since you have tried a new grain, a different bean, or an unusual vegetable. If you have tried quinoa, millet, or amaranth; Anasazi, Cherokee wax, or black turtle beans; Jerusalem artichokes, yellow mangles, or purple Cherokee tomatoes—you are ahead of the pack! The rest of us need to adopt more flexibility.

Most of the world depends on wheat and rice as their main staples. Vast acreages are planted in these crops, worldwide. As more and more farmers adopted these crops, the genetic diversity of our food diminished. Pests and diseases love these large fields planted in a single crop. Farmers fight back with chemicals, using more and more to produce the same amount of food. Meanwhile, we are losing a vast amount of adaptability by relying on so few crops. Our food supply will be seriously challenged if weather or climate changes enough to give the pests and diseases the upper hand. Buying and growing a large variety of unprocessed foods, encourages diversity and adaptability in farms and gardens. The more diversity we have in our food crops the more food secure we will be.

Flexibility when buying in bulk is also very helpful to the budget.

When everyone is waiting in line for rice, buy barley instead. When wheat prices are high, stock up on triticale (a cross between rye and wheat). No dry fava beans this year? Lima beans might make an acceptable substitute. Grains and beans store for at least two years when you take good care of them. Buying when the price is right helps smooth out the budget.

Experiment with new foods before you stock up. (The Internet is a good place to find recipes.) You don't want to buy 25 pounds of white kidney beans—only to discover that you don't really care for them. While every new food may not please everyone, trying new foods can become a family tradition.

A decade or so ago, I ran a small child development center in a rural mountain community. We had preschoolers all day and older kids after school. We provided snacks, and each week I made a habit of getting them something new to try. At first only a few kids dared to try what I had brought them, but soon that changed. As the other children saw the delight on the faces of their brave and flexible peers, they soon decided to be brave and flexible too. Within a month of having something new for snack each week, the kids would hound me on my shopping day. They wanted to know what their new surprise food was. We started having meetings before I went shopping, so they could vote on which foods they wanted to have again. They loved aronia berry juice, dried cherries, sweet potato chips, blue corn tortillas, and many other foods most kids never have at day care, or even at home. These kids were mostly from meat and potatoes kinds of households. If they could get excited about new foods, I am sure you can too.

Flexible eating habits help support the crop diversity that contributes to world food security. Flexible bulk shopping allows you to buy when the price is right. Shopping flexible, is shopping wise. While we are on the subject of shopping for food, we don't want to forget about feeding our immune system. That is the subject of the next chapter.

13. Don't Forget Your Immune System

When planning for long term storage and emergency caches, don't forget to think about your immune system. Many of the world's health organizations are already worried about pandemics. They probably aren't even considering the complications related to food shortages, climate change, or crop failures. Students of history know that most serious food shortages (referred to as famines) are followed by disease and plague. When folks live close together and their nutrition is inadequate, it's a formula for disaster.

Many people depend on Vitamin C, garlic, Echinacea, Oregon grape-root, and shiitake mushrooms to keep their immune systems in tip top shape. More information each of these is coming right up. For sustainability, growing immune system boosters is easy; tips are included with each listing beginning below.

Vitamin C: There are lots of choices and you may already have a favorite supplement or food source. For those who don't, here's some information on a couple of popular supplements. (Food sources are covered in the next paragraph). "Emergen-C" comes in convenient packets and it makes a fizzing drink that tastes good enough. It's great for those times you feel you need a little immunity boost, but you don't think your stomach will let you swallow a pill. "Ester-C," another popular type, is widely available as tablets and pills. Both of these forms of Vitamin C are non-acidic and contain minerals that boost their effectiveness. I keep some of both in my pantry and emergency caches. Read the instructions on the package, and don't exceed the recommended dosage.

For sustainable Vitamin C, there are a number of options. Citrus trees, such as lemons, limes, oranges, tangerines, and grapefruit are good sources of Vitamin C. In addition to full sized trees, miniature, dwarf, and indoor varieties are offered in catalogs and on the Internet. Rose hips, especially from Rosa rugosa and R. canina are additional good sources, and they will grow in colder climates. Rose hips are tasty made into jam when fresh, and they can be dried for tea. Berries of many kinds are also high in Vitamin C. Check out local nurseries, mail order catalogs and search on-line. Choose varieties of citrus, berries, and rose hips that ripen at different times, to stretch your Vitamin C season as long as possible.

Garlic is often in the news for its myriad health benefits. It is easy to grow, fresh garlic is available almost everywhere, and you can find it in capsule or pill form as a dietary supplement. The garlic offered as a supplement has a fairly long shelf life, so it makes a good addition to emergency caches. Use it as directed on the label.

For sustainability, you can grow garlic in containers or in the ground. It is generally planted (from cloves) in October, in most temperate zones. It will grow until the ground freezes, or is covered in snow, and then begin growing again in spring. If you missed the fall planting season, get it into the ground as soon as you can in the spring. Instead of cloves you may have round onion shaped bulbs by fall. Any of these round garlic bulbs that you don't use over the next winter can be replanted the following spring. By the next fall you should have classic garlic cloves. Save some to plant each year and you will have garlic forever. Unless you have gophers; gophers love garlic. If they are a problem, be sure to plant the garlic in containers.

Home grown and store bought garlic are both great for flavoring foods, either raw or cooked. Raw garlic is reported to have the best immune enhancing properties. Dice or press fresh garlic on to soup or salad whenever you feel you need an immune enhancing boost.

Echinacea is a beautiful easy to grow flower that is perfectly happy in almost any sunny spot. Hungry gophers will devour it, just like garlic, so if they are a problem plant it in containers. For medicinal use, seek out the species (Echinacea purpurea, E. angustifolia, and/or E. pallidia) rather than hybrids or cultivars. Steep fresh Echinacea flowers or leaves for an immune enhancing tea (technically called an infusion) for those times you feel you need a boost.

Dried, the petals and leaves can be stored for up to nine months. For longer storage, purchase the dried roots as capsules, powder, or cut for tea. Once your plants are well established, you can also dig your own Echinacea roots to dry. Divide the plants in fall and dry any portions you don't replant. To make more plants, you can start from seed. The mature dry flower heads will contain viable seeds. Allow them to self-sow, or plant the seeds in flats and expose them to outdoor temperatures over the winter, they should germinate by late spring.

Echinacea is a powerful medicine and should only be used, as needed, for short periods of times. Read the section on ***Herb Safety*** near the end of the next chapter to learn how to determine if this is the right herb for you.

Cayenne and Chili Peppers: While you may not appreciate hot peppers, the hotter they are, the more medicinal they are considered. Peppers contain Vitamin C, anti-oxidants, and phyto-nutrients. They can pick you up when you are feeling sluggish and they help clear congestion. The spice and seasoning racks found in most grocery stores can supply you with cayenne and chili powder. Dried whole peppers are often sold in stores that specialize in bulk, gourmet, and ethnic foods. Cayenne is available at most health food stores and herb shops, in capsules, for its many health enhancing properties. Dried whole peppers, the powdered packaged spice, or capsules—can be stored in emergency caches and in a kitchen cupboard or pantry. Use common sense and moderation when ingesting peppers. If you over-do it you won't soon forget the burn that keeps on giving.

Peppers are easy to grow in the summer garden. The seeds need warmth to germinate and the plants take a long time to mature. Unless you live in zone ten or higher, they need to be started early, in a sunny window or green house. You can plant them out in the garden after the threat of frost has passed. Seeds found in mature dry peppers can be saved for growing the following year.

Shiitake Mushrooms offer gourmet flavor and immune enhancing benefits. Costco and other "large box" stores often have gallon sized containers of dried shiitakes at bargain prices. Many health food stores and herb shops have shiitake mushrooms as immune enhancing capsules. These capsules will take up far less space in emergency caches. However, they can be pricey, which may be a consideration. Almost any book on Chinese herbs will have a chapter on shiitake mushrooms. You can also look for clinical research results by searching on the Internet.

Shiitake mushrooms are fun to grow at home. Kits are offered by many mail order garden catalogs. For those who have woodland or forested property, plugs are available to inoculate hard wood logs. Once the logs have started producing mushrooms, plugs can be cut from one end to inoculate other logs for the next batch. If this is something that interests you, do some research on forest farming—either on the Internet or at the local library.

Oregon Grape is a good herb to have in the garden and emergency caches. It is easy to grow, and it has the same active principals as the well known herb, golden seal. Golden seal is endangered in the wild and difficult to grow in the home garden; Oregon grape is a superior substitute. Oregon grape is considered anti-biotic, anti-fungal, and anti-viral. It's not used as a food or an everyday tea. But when your body is fighting off an attack of some kind, it may be exactly what you need. Steep or boil the leaves to make tea. An even stronger tea is made by chopping and boiling the stems or roots.

Oregon grape is available as capsules and as a bulk herb—from health food stores and herb shops. I keep capsules on hand at home, as well as dried leaves, and use it whenever I feel a virus or infection coming on. Many people use the powdered root externally on wounds, mild infections, and cold sores. This powerful herb should be used sparingly and avoided during pregnancy. See the section on ***Herb Safety*** at the end of the next chapter to learn how to find important and individualized information on using herbs.

Salt has many therapeutic uses! Gargling and swishing with warm salty water is an old time remedy for simple sore throats and minor mouth irritations. Soaking minor cuts, scrapes, and sprains in warm salty water can bring relief from irritation as well as stave off infection. A good supply of salt is useful for long term storage and emergency caches. (Though not subject to insect infestation, it will need stored in an airtight container so it doesn't absorb moisture from the air.)

Salt sustainability is a bit of a challenge, unless you live near the ocean, a salt water lake, or an inland source of salt deposits. If a source of salt is near-by, processing it is easier than you might think. Starting with salt water, it is first allowed to settle in a large pot or other container. Any material that floats to the top is discarded. The settled water is then dipped out, leaving behind any sediment, and poured through a fine mesh strainer or a few layers of cheese cloth, and turned into salt crystals by evaporation or boiling.

If you are starting with dry land salt deposits, you will want to contact your state's Geological Survey office to get information on the other minerals present in the salt. If it doesn't contain significant amounts of a toxic mineral, say, uranium or mercury, find out if you need to apply for a mining claim to utilize it. Natural salt deposits are simply ground up and used as they are, or if they contain impurities, they are dissolved in water and then processed like salt water. Processing it like salt water will not remove toxic minerals; however, it will help remove rocks, sand, dirt, and organic matter.

Salt was once a valuable trade item, and it may become one again. If you live near a source of natural salt, you might want to mull over the possibilities when you get to Chapter 25, **Rethinking Economies and Careers**. (Natural regional salts are actually in demand now. You may not have to wait for non-renewable resources to dwindle before it is economically feasible to market local salt.)

Historically, people in regions that lacked both a source of salt, and trade partners that could supply it, had a number of strategies to supply minerals to their diets. These generally involved using other types of mineral deposits, plants that concentrate minerals, or using the ashes from various plants that were burned in open fires or incinerated in narrow mouthed ceramic vessels.

While information on these processes is not easy to find, here are some tips, just in case you are interested. Look for local ethno-botany, indigenous, and primitive skills classes. These classes may give information about plants or mineral deposits that you can use as a substitute for salt. While these substitutes may not be as effective against infections, they should provide a reasonable source of sodium and other minerals. *An Ethnobiology Source Book*, edited by Richard I. Ford and published by Garland, contains a lot of useful information for many US regions. Your local university library may have a copy in its collections. You may find more information on processing salt (or salt substitutes) through natural history centers and historical societies, either of which may have classes, articles, or books covering the process.

Local Medicinal Plants: Learning about local wild medicinal plants should turn up a number of other herbs you can use to enhance immune function. Watch for classes in the calendar section of your local newspapers and alternative publications. Many state and national parks, museums, and colleges offer periodic classes. Local herb stores and nature centers are other places to ask. Also check the ***Educational Opportunities*** section of Chapter 27, **More Resources**, near the end of this book. Several organizations that offer ethno-botany and medicinal plant classes are listed. Libraries and bookstores often have titles covering local medicinal plants; however, before you ingesting any plant material, always confirm plant identification with a knowledgeable person. You will also want to get informed about local poisonous plants, so you don't make a deadly mistake. Lists of toxic and poisonous plants are available in many books and on-line. Ask at your local library or bookstore or search on: your region / poisonous plants. For more information also see the section on ***Herb Safety*** at the bottom of the next chapter, **Other Essential Herbs**.

General Herb Information: Dried herbs and herbal products are available at many health and natural food stores. Some communities have herb shops and other herbal suppliers can also be found on-line. (One reliable source is Richter's Herbs, listed in the ***Sources for Gardeners*** section of Chapter 27, **More Resources**.) Be sure to check the expiration dates on any tinctures, capsules, dried bulk herbs, or vitamins that you plan to purchase. If the label or bulk container doesn't give the expiration date, ask the staff or shop keeper how long the herbs can be stored. Add a notation to your notebook, so you can keep track of expiration dates. (See ***Shelf Life***, Chapter 7, **Storing Staples Securely**.)

Any herbs that aren't adequately prepackaged will need to be repackaged and stored just like other staples.

Next we are going to take a look at a few other herbs you might want to purchase, recognize, or grow, to round out your ability to care for your family just in case, one day, the doctors are no longer available.

14. Other Essential Herbs

The following herbs will get you started with simple comforting remedies for all sorts of circumstances. To keep the listings brief I have used medicinal action terms to describe the common uses of these plants. You will find a list of these terms with definitions, information on preparations, obtaining herbs, ***Wild Crafting***, and ***Herb Safety***—at the end of the herb listings.

American Ephedra is used for water balance; the urinary, reproductive, and respiratory systems; as an antidepressant; for allergic reactions; and to relieve minor aches and pains. Ephedra is prepared as a decoction. It is reported to be diuretic, febrifuge, and tonic. Herb books list it as "Desert Tea," "Mormon Tea," "Indian Tea," or even "Squaw Tea." Native people call it "Stick Tea," or simply "tea."

Cleavers helps with elimination. The infusion is considered cleansing to the blood and nervous system. Cleavers is useful for chronic congestion, and it is included as part of many weight loss formulas. The infusion is used both internally and externally (as a fomentation) for painful muscles and joints. Cleavers are often listed as "Bedstraw" or "Gallium" in herb books and they are reportedly antispasmodic, diaphoretic, depurative, diuretic, and vulnerary.

Comfrey is one herb plant that I am never without. It stimulates healing and reduces swelling and pain when used as a poultice on sprains and bruises. Comfrey should not be used internally by young children, the elderly, or those with inadequate digestive enzymes—in fact the FDA considers it unsafe for internal use, no matter what. Comfrey is reportedly anodyne, astringent, demulcent, expectorant, hemostatic, and vulnerary.

Fennel has many uses. A weak infusion is very soothing for stomach ache. It also soothes the nerves and relieves pain. A decoction is said to stimulate mother's milk and many find it balancing to the female system. It is considered safe for pregnancy, excellent for morning sickness, and helpful for symptoms of menopause. Fennel is listed as antispasmodic, carminative, digestive, diuretic, and expectorant.

Mint makes a welcome addition to most any herb mixture. It improves the flavor and is believed to improve the effectiveness of other remedies. It is used for stomach aches, headaches, coughs, congestion, and as a part of liver tonics. Mint is considered anodyne, antispasmodic, carminative, cholagogue, digestive, febrifuge, and tonic.

Mullein is a favorite remedy around my home, both for its expectorant qualities and its ability to soothe the nerves. It is usually made into an infusion, which is served either hot or iced, with or without the addition of a little honey. Mullein is reportedly anodyne, antispasmodic, demulcent, diuretic, and vulnerary.

White Willow is used for the same purposes many people use aspirin. In addition it has been employed for allergic reactions and to relieve muscle tension. Willow is listed as anodyne, antiseptic, astringent, diaphoretic, diuretic, febrifuge, and tonic. Commonly prepared as an infusion; willow has a bitter taste, and benefits from being mixed with mint and sweetened with honey.

Yellow Dock root decoction makes an excellent gentle laxative. It is also traditionally used to build and purify the blood. The root, tinctured in vinegar, is my favorite remedy for athlete's foot. The leaves are edible and tasty. All parts of the plant contain oxalic acid, so they should be used internally in moderation. Yellow Dock is considered cholagogue, depurative, laxative, and tonic.

Yerba Santa is one of the best remedies for respiratory ailments and simple stomach aches. This herb makes a pleasant infusion when combined with mint, cleavers, and/or mullein. Yerba Santa is reportedly antispasmodic, expectorant, febrifuge, and tonic.

Basic Information on Using Herbs

Herbal Preparations

Decoction: Tea prepared by simmering two tablespoons dried herb in one quart of water for twenty minutes, unless otherwise directed.

Fomentation: A cloth soaked in herb tea and placed on the skin, sometimes over an achy joint or muscle.

Infusion: Tea prepared by placing a teaspoon of dried herbs in a cup or mug and carefully pouring in a cup of boiling water. Steep until cool enough to drink and then strain if desired.

Tincture: Place ½ cup dried herb in a clean pint canning jar, cover with vinegar or vodka, store in a cool dark location for several weeks, and shake when you remember.

Poultice: Pound approximately one cup of fresh herbs until moist, and place on the skin or over an achy joint or muscle. You can cover the poultice with plastic wrap and an ace bandage, so you can move around, but resting is probably part of the cure.

Medicinal Actions

Anodyne: Soothes and relives pain.

Antiseptic: Prevents infection by destroying or inhibiting bacteria.

Antispasmodic: Relieves spasms, cramps, and muscular tension.

Astringent: Contracts tissues and dries excessive moisture.

Carminative: Useful for relieving gas pains, both in the stomach and the intestines.

Cholagogue: Increases the flow of bile.

Demulcent: Soothes irritated tissue—including the urinary tract, respiratory system, mucous membranes, the digestive tract, and the lining of the joints.

Depurative: Cleans the blood.

Digestive: Aids digestion.

Diaphoretic: Promotes perspiration, opens pores, and reduces fever.

Diuretic: Relieves water retention, bloating, and increases urination.

Expectorant: Helps eliminate mucus from the respiratory tract.

Febrifuge: Reduces fever.

Hemostatic (sometimes spelled **Haemostatic**): Stops bleeding.

Laxative: Relieves constipation.

Tonic: Strengthens and invigorates the body or specific organs.

Vulnerary: Used externally to heal wounds.

Wild Crafting

Wild Crafting refers to the art of collecting food and medicine from wild plants. A lot of thought and care needs to go into the process. You don't want to take so much from any plant, or group of plants, that they won't regenerate; and you must avoid areas that are contaminated. Be extra careful with plant identification—you don't want to accidently gather something toxic. Many herb books and web sites explore these topics in depth. You can also find more information in my herb book *Sacred Smoke, The Ancient Art of Smudging for Modern Times*, published by Native Voices, and available from on-line book outlets or by request from most libraries and book stores.

Herb Safety

Most herbs are safer than over the counter and prescription medicines, but that doesn't mean you shouldn't be careful. Always do some research before using any medicinal substance, even those prescribed by a doctor. Using the Internet, start by searching for side effects, i.e.: Fennel / Side effects. Next search for information related to your personal health challenges, i.e.: Fennel / Diabetes. Last but not least, search for drug and herb interactions, i.e.: Fennel / Interactions. You can also search on specific interactions, i.e.: Fennel / Aspirin / Interactions. Many libraries have public Internet access, volunteers to help those new to the Internet, or referrals to other organizations that offer classes.

Herbs by Mail Order

If you don't have a local or favorite herb outlet, see Richter's Herbs, listed in the ***Sources for Gardeners*** section of Chapter 27, **More Resources.** They have a large selection of herbs, many of which are available as dry herbs, herbal preparations, seeds, and plants.

More Information

My favorite herb book is titled simply enough: *The Herb Book*. It was written by John Lust, and is now published by Benedict Lust Productions. Another popular title is *Back to Eden*, by Jethro Kloss, published by Lotus Press. Back to Eden was my very first herb book, and it still has a place on my bookshelf.

Next we will be looking beyond food and herbs, at other items you will need for your emergency caches.

15. Additional Items for Emergency Caches

Emergency caches need to contain everything necessary to utilize the food you have stored. Once you have a food list together, think through preparation and cooking. Consider different weather and disaster scenarios. What if there is a flood? (You may need dry kindling and newspaper or a camp stove and fuel.) What if the fire danger is very high, it's raining, or windy? (Cooking areas will need to be sheltered.) Go through all the probable scenarios and make sure you have the minimum supplies necessary stored in or near the emergency cache. Below you will find some suggestions. Some of these supplies have expiration dates. Check the labels and log expiration dates in your notebook so you can cycle perishable items out of the caches for use in the house before they expire. (See ***Shelf Life***, Chapter 7, **Storing Staples Securely.**)

For cooking, you will need a couple of cooking pots (in addition to those for boiling water) and wooden spoons for stirring and serving food. Other necessities include a can opener (not electric), a sturdy multi-purpose knife, and a wet-stone to keep it sharpened. You will also need a good supply of matches or a fire starting kit (see ***Fire Making*** in Chapter 22, **Useful Skills**). A BBQ, or at least a grate that you can use over a small fire pit scooped out of the dirt, will help keep cooking fires contained. If dry firewood may be hard to come by, a camp stove with plenty of fuel canisters is a good idea.

Don't forget eating utensils. One cup, plate, fork, and spoon per person are sufficient. Sturdy, shatter resistant plastic for plates, and stainless forks and spoons are a good idea. You will find ideas for replacing the plastic as it wears out, in Chapter 22, **Useful Skills**.

Other items that can help with disaster survival are rain gear, thermal blankets, sturdy shoes or boots, sturdy gloves and work clothes for clean-up work, as well as warm gloves, hats, and other clothing for cold weather. For hot weather you may want sunscreen, sunglasses with UV protection, hats or baseball caps, mosquito netting, light weight clothing, and bug repellent. Let's not think about whole wardrobes, just the very basics. Also include a small sewing kit that contains a number of different sized needles and different weights of thread, so you can repair different types of material.

Personal care products don't take up much room: tooth brushes, tooth paste, floss, fingernail clippers, a comb or brush, and any hygiene or feminine products you require. Those with life saving prescriptions can ask their doctors about including these medicines in their caches. Also look for all purpose supplies, like Dr. Bronner's Castile Soap, which is good for the body, hair, dishes, clothes, and other cleaning needs. I use tea tree oil for bites, minor cuts, irritation, and inflammation, so I packed some in both my emergency caches. Check expiration dates on sunscreen, toothpaste, and other similar products. Log expiration dates in your notebook and cycle perishable items out of caches before they expire. (See ***Shelf Life***, Chapter 7, **Storing Staples Securely**.)

Be prepared to fend for yourself after a disaster. (If you think someone else is going to look out for you, just ask the folks who survived Katrina how much help they got from FEMA and the Red Cross. I don't really mean to be so alarmist, but we all need a reality check here. I once lived in a house that burnt to the ground. The fire department instructed me to wait for Red Cross. They never showed up. I don't think the situation I faced, or those who survived Katrina, is all that unusual.) In the interest of being independent, store general utility items; a hammer and nails, rope and twine, or other similar materials that you know how to use. Seeds to plant a garden, as well as a trowel, some light weight pruners, and a shovel may also be a good idea. Do some brainstorming with family and friends and add anything else you can't live without or that will improve your quality of life. You may be able to provide a better life for yourself than you would have in a refugee camp. However, if it's safer to relocate and you have the opportunity, the seeds and supplies will be useful—where ever you are.

A well stocked first aid kit is always a good idea, as well as a book on first aid. While I may not have a lot of faith in the Red Cross as far as their emergency services go, their first aid books and training are top notch. The Red Cross publishes *First Aid Fast*, available on the publications page of their web site: <http://www.redcross.org/pubs/>. (While you are there, look for the information on community disaster education.) Once you have a first aid book in hand, you can plan purchases for an effective kit. You want to have small, but adequate, kits in or near living areas, emergency caches, and cars, as well as a more complete kit in the house, garage, or shed. Take steps to protect these supplies from insects, rodents, moisture, excessive heat, and freezing. Don't forget to check for expiration dates on antiseptic and other similar supplies.

Keep a well stocked disaster kit in your car or other vehicle(s). Include water, matches and newspaper, a sturdy knife, a blanket or sleeping bag, sturdy shoes, prepackaged snacks that don't need preparation, and season appropriate items from the previous paragraphs. Stock your vehicle(s) with flares and a flashlight, a tire pressure gauge, a spare tire, a jack (that actually works for your vehicle), a tire iron (that matches the lugs on your wheels), a can or two of spare air, extra fuses, a first aid kit, a small bucket and shovel, and whatever else you can think of that will be helpful. I could tell you a story about what it is like to have the wrong jack and the wrong tire iron—when you are alone, in the dark, on a lonely dirt road high in the mountains. (Oh, by the way, the snacks, water, and sleeping bag did come in handy. So did the hiking boots, I had to walk out and get help the following day.) One more little thing, always keep your ID and credit card in your pocket, even when you are headed into remote areas. I had a heck of a time getting money out of the bank when I couldn't prove who I was.

OK, enough reminiscing, let's get back to the task at hand. A signaling devise for vehicles and emergency caches is essential. Pocket sized sirens and other electronic devices are popular, but an old fashioned whistle should work as well. Whistles are versatile. You can learn or develop simple codes to communicate with family, and if someone is searching for survivors—a whistle can save your life. Whistles don't need batteries, you can blow them much longer and louder than you can yell, and they are pretty dang cheap too. So buy a few, and keep them with your emergency gear.

Now, ask me, "Honestly, Harvest, do you have all this stuff stashed in your emergency caches?" Well, the fact is, no. Will I be sorry? Maybe. I am working on my caches a little at a time. You can do the same thing. Make up a list, and each pay check try to add something to your caches or long term storage supplies. Having a space limit is a good idea. There are tons of things we buy that we can really comfortably live without. Besides, purchasing excessive stuff contributes to carbon emissions, which is part of what got the planet in this mess to begin with. So, buy what you need, but keep it to a minimum. Stay tuned, Chapter 17, **Your Food Storage Plan,** will help fine tune your food choices. In Chapter 18 we will get everything packed and cached in as secure a spot as possible.

Now, while we are considering extra items for caches, I am going to ask you to consider not buying a gun to protect your cache. Guns often cause harm and they may be less useful than you imagine. Why you should forget about handguns is the subject of the next chapter.

16. Forget About Guns

I know many people are including firearms and ammunition in their food security plans. Before you take this step, think about the old saying, "He, who lives by the sword, dies by the sword." The same thought can be applied to guns. I think there are worse things than dying by the gun. I think living by the gun would be pretty close to life on a hot inhospitable planet populated with creatures of evil intent. In fact, it would be worse. With a gun in your hand and fear in your heart, terrible things could happen. Terrible things that you would have to live with until, perhaps, you died by the gun.

Many people from many different traditions see bad times ahead. They are worried about hungry hoards roaming the countryside desperate for food. Perhaps they are right. Some of these people may be armed. Let's think this through. If a hungry person shows up at my door someday, with a gun in hand, it is my hope that I can invite them to eat at my table with grace. "Brother, please put your gun away. We can get you something to eat. Then, if you are willing to do a share of the work, you can help us keep everyone fed."

Nature is incredibly abundant. Today, I spent a couple of hours clipping perfectly edible plants into small pieces to use for mulch. These plants were volunteers (meaning they planted themselves), and I have way more than I need. I probably clipped up enough greens for the vegetable portion of three big kettles of soup. There's lots of wild grain in the fields near me, and there are cottonwood, locust, and pine trees. Do you remember Euell Gibbons? He was famous for saying: "Ever eat a pine tree? Many parts are edible." Well, many plants and trees commonly found in yards and neighborhoods are edible; and gardens are truly amazing. I have moderate disabilities and a small garden. Last summer eight different households had a share of my produce.

What about hunting? If you already own a rifle or shotgun, and are proficient; stock up on ammunition. Ammunition is on the list of things that going to get more expensive and possibly be in short supply. Metal is not a renewable resource. Only a certain amount was ever in the ground, and according to many accounts the ore is nearly mined out. Once out of the ground and refined, metal doesn't last forever. It corrodes, fatigues, and eventually turns to rust. It takes a lot of energy to mine and refine the metal for shell casings. Right now that energy comes from fossil fuels, another nonrenewable resource. If that wasn't enough bad news, the potassium used to make gun powder is also non-renewable. The US has already depleted its stores and now relies on imports. I have already heard complaints, from local hunters, about the declining quality of bullets. This trend is likely to continue.

Archery is a worthy option. For sustainable hunting supplies you can learn to make bows and arrows. (Classes are offered through the Miwok Archeological Preserve. For contact information see the ***Educational Opportunities*** section of Chapter 27, **More Resources**.)

Nature is incredibly abundant. Forget the guns. Grow a garden and learn about wild foods. (Euell Gibbons is the author of several books on edible plants.) Desperate people do desperate things. Forgive them for not knowing any better and welcome them with grace. If you attract a few refugees, put them to work processing and storing food. If civilization falls apart, there will be plenty of work for everyone to do.

17. Your Food Storage Plan

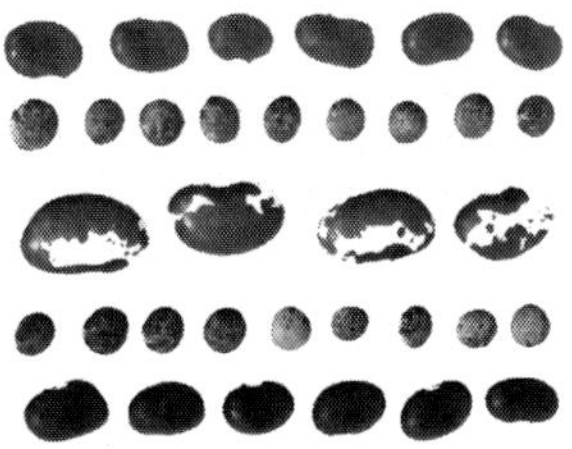

Each family has different eating habits and needs, so food storage plans need to be unique. To help you understand the basics of putting a plan together, I am going to start out using myself as an example. My diet is primarily grains and beans, plus fresh vegetables from the garden, and local fruit. If you look back over Chapter 10, **Balance is Everything**, you will see that this simple diet provides for most of our nutritional needs.

Taking a closer look, starting with complex carbohydrates, in my diet these are primarily from whole grains and dry beans. I was purchasing approximately five pounds of grain and beans a month, divided between a number of different types (both for variety and to encourage diversity). A little simple arithmetic shows I need sixty pounds of grains and beans to last a year.

Your complex carbohydrates may come from whole grain pasta, bread, crackers; or root vegetables—such as potatoes. Make a list of the carbohydrate foods you eat, and then look over the lists of foods in Chapter 8, **Wise Food Choices for Storage**, to see which foods can be stored. Estimate how much your family uses of these foods in a week or a month (adding extra, if necessary, to compensate for foods you eat that can't be stored). Multiply that by the number of weeks or months you want to store food, and you are ready to get started on a shopping list.

Continue working down the list of dietary needs in Chapter 10, **Balance is Everything.** Double check what you normally eat, against the information in Chapter 8, **Wise Food Choices for Storage**, as well as Chapter 9, **Poor Choices for Food Storage**. The main idea is to figure out your source of nutrients, decide what you need to store, and calculate how much you will need. Keep sustainability in mind. Whole grains and beans can be planted to produce more food. Pasta and canned potatoes won't grow.

If you're not used to cooking from scratch or using whole unprocessed foods, I recommend the book: *Animal, Vegetable, Miracle*, by Barbara Kingsolver, which is listed in the ***Recommended Reading*** section of Chapter 27, **More Resources**. This book elegantly shows how to place homemade family meals back in the center of our often busy lives. I am sure you will find it inspiring.

Those who garden or know about wild foods may not feel the need to store many fruits or vegetables. For instance, my garden is full of veggies all year long and I know about wild local foods. However, in addition to my stored grains and beans, I have a pantry stocked with a nice selection of home processed fruit preserves, pickles, and other assorted home canned goods. Having all this food is great, and not just for emergencies.

I recently had a houseful of unexpected company. The Indigenous Permaculture Program came to our small community to present some workshops, and our air quality was poor because of forest fires. Camping out was not really a good option, so I invited the presenters to stay at my place. I ended up preparing lunch for fifteen people, two days in a row. I made soup with red beans and garden vegetables one day, and black beans with sautéed vegetables on the side the next. On both days I made a pot of mixed grain pilaf and a raw vegetable platter. We had fresh berries from the garden and cherries from a friend's orchard. I was left feeling very gracious and bountiful. Having plenty to share, without worrying about having enough for your family is a wonderful feeling. Stocking up is not only for emergencies!

Once you come up with a list of what you want to store, check local sources first. Many natural food stores have bulk supplies available, as do big box stores like Costco and Sam's Club. (I recently found a great buy at my closest Costco. I purchased a couple of 12 pound bags of organic short grain brown rice, that was grown within 100 miles of my home, and it was about half the price of the conventionally grown rice sold on-line!)

Tips on finding local sources can be found in Chapter 5, **Food Security 101**. Look for the web addresses for sites listing CSA's and the WWOOF web site. Another good web site for finding local farms is: <http://www.localharvest.org/>. Don't forget to check out local farmers markets. They are good sources of local quality foods. To find a farmers market near you, use the search function on this handy web page from the USDA: <http://apps.ams.usda.gov/FarmersMarkets/>.

Food buying clubs are a good way to buy bulk foods at reasonable costs. Unfortunately, there is not a single web site that offers a directory of food buying clubs. Use the Internet to search on "food buying clubs." Tons of sites come up, sort through them to find a club near you. Starting a food buying club is also a possibility. *The Food Conspiracy Cookbook: How to Start a Neighborhood Food Buying Club*, by Lois Wickstrom, will get you off to a good start. (Unfortunately, this book is out of print. However, it is available through many libraries and at reasonable prices from used book sellers.)

If local suppliers, farmers, or food buying clubs don't work out for you, you can always buy on line. One reliable source is Bob's Red Mill: <http://www.bobsredmill.com/>.

After your storage plan is organized and implemented, it will be time to think about keeping it stocked up. Chapter 19, **Food Security and Your Garden** will get you started on producing some of your own supplies.

Until then you can make a bulk purchase or two each month to ensure on-going supplies—or you might want to join a CSA. (See Chapter 5, **Food Security 101**, for more information on Community Supported Agriculture.)

Now that the long term storage plan is dialed in, we are ready to think about packing our emergency caches. That is the subject of the next chapter.

18. Packing the Emergency Cache

Be creative! Think outside the box; as well as inside the can, pan, and pot. The purpose of the emergency cache is to keep you and your family supplied while the flood waters recede, the fire burns out, or the ground stops shaking. However, you don't need to stash all your supplies in one container or in one exact spot. I am going to describe some of the thinking involved in my own emergency caches, to help you get started thinking about your own.

The first step is to outline the most obvious threats: I live in a floodplain. I know it is not ideal, but here I am. There is also a significant threat of fire where I live, as well as earthquakes. If you are not sure what possible threats may face your region, Chapter 6, **Location, Location, Location** will help you evaluate the risks. To address the risks in my area, I have two emergency caches. One is buried in the back yard, in case of fire or earthquakes; the other is in the attic over the garage, in case of flooding.

Let's take a look at the cached buried in the back yard. I considered the potential sources of fuel for fires and falling debris (from a fire or earthquake) and sited my cache accordingly. We are not located right on a fault, in which case, I may have had to think twice about burying the cache. Being in the floodplain, where the land is nice and flat, I don't have to think about landslides as much as those who live on sloping ground.

The buried cache is packed into two large stock pots and a small metal garbage can. They are duct taped closed and slipped into two garbage bags, one up and one down, to keep both rain and ground water from seeping in. Water filtering supplies (for back-packers, from the sporting goods store), a small amount of food, a cooking pot, wooden spoon, knife, hot pads, a hand pruner for gathering wild food and medicine, fire starting supplies, a flash light, a water proof tarp, a couple of blankets, a first aid kit, a couple of bowls, forks, and spoons, and that's it. Those with strong backs, who don't mind digging—might want a change of clothes, rain gear, and sleeping bags; especially where large quakes are a possibility.

My other emergency cache, in the attic of the garage, addresses the fact that I live in the floodplain. The floor of the garage attic is solid wood planks, much more secure than the sheet rock ceiling in the house. The plank floor in the garage makes it a better site than the attic in house for two reasons. First, as you already know, we are in an earthquake region. If a heavy garbage can full of emergency supplies were to fall over on the sheetrock ceiling, it might fall right through and cause serious injury. Secondly, the plank floor in the garage attic makes a much safer and more comfortable refuge to wait out flood waters or rescue.

In the attic, all my individual containers are stored inside metal garbage cans, and each container is wrapped in either cloth or newspaper for insulation. The garbage cans are duct taped closed, to help keep out moisture, rodents, and insects. Since the attic is subject to temperature changes, the food and other perishables are rotated out every few months, to avoid rancidity and spoilage.

Besides food and water, and water filtering and boiling supplies, there is a camp stove, a kerosene heater, fuel, a couple of lighters, flash flights, small battery powered radio (and extra batteries), a whistle for signaling, minimal cooking supplies, air mattresses and a foot pump, towels, changes of clothes, and a couple of sleeping bags. I have a few tools, a small collection of garden seeds, a first aid kit, and some plastic bags for collecting wild foods. The main idea is to get by until the water recedes or evacuation happens. I suppose some sort of raft or boat is a good idea. I will have to add that to my list.

Think creatively when planning cache(s). Gather family or other team members together to discuss what to include and where to place the cache(s). Your list of supplies, where you store them, and how you protect them from the elements and other hazards may not resemble mine. Apply the following basics for each emergency cache: place it in a spot it is likely to survive the disaster(s) it is planned for; mark it in some way so you can find it; keep track of the expiration dates on the food, personal care, and first aid supplies. These things should be rotated out of your caches and replaced on a regular basis.

Disaster preparedness only begins with your emergency cache, when you come across articles and radio or television programs—pay attention. We can always learn more, and it may help us keep our families safe. Next we will be moving beyond emergency preparation to take a look at the role gardens can play in family food security.

19. Food Security and the Garden

Working in the garden is medicine for all of life's woes. Gardening is wonderful therapy for stress, it's good exercise, and it helps with the family food budget. You don't even have a yard to reap all the benefits of gardening. You can start with containers in a bright window or on a porch or patio. Soon, you may want enough space to dig in the dirt. Perhaps family members, friends, or close neighbors have a spot available. Community gardens are another option, and they are fun places to meet other gardeners. Call your local chamber of commerce, community center, or library and ask about community gardens in the area. If after making some calls you still haven't found a spot, it is time to turn to the Internet. Many community gardens, in the USA and Canada, are listed on the American Community Garden Association's web page: <http://www.communitygarden.org/>. They also have tips for getting new gardens started.

Community gardens are great places for novice gardeners to learn the ropes. They often have meetings where you can get to know other gardeners. Once you have a plot, you can also learn a lot by showing up at the garden with tools and seeds or plants. Feel free to ask other gardeners for advice. If no one is around, follow the instruction on the seed package or plant label. While it is nice to be mentored, the best gardening education is earned through trial and error. Seedlings and young plants are like babies, they need tender loving care. Provide them with plenty of moisture until they can sink their roots deep in the soil. Once established they can stand a little neglect.

Be sure to grow some of your family's favorite foods. That way gardening will become a pleasure; not simply another chore. Flowers have their place, and not just for the beauty they bring. Many flowering plants attract beneficial insects; which will help keep the pests under control. Include a few plants with wonderful velvety textures and some that are fragrant. Don't forget your favorite seasonings, such as dill, cilantro, or rosemary. Food, mealtime, and gardening should please all the senses.

When you have made gardening part of the pleasure of life, it is time to broaden the scope of the garden. Take a look at the produce you still purchase, and try growing more of those things. Other good plants to consider produce food that's saved for winter. Flour corn, winter squash, and dry beans are good choices for beginners. Many root crops, such as potatoes, carrots, and turnips also provide cold weather fare.

Each region has peculiarities to climate, soil, and water. Regional day and night time temperatures, the temperature of the soil, the pH of the soil and water, and many other factors determine which vegetables and fruit will thrive for you. In areas with short growing seasons, timing is critical. An experienced garden mentor can shorten the learning curve. (If no one is available to take you under their wing, see Chapter 27, **More Resources**—look in the ***On the Web*** section for Cornell University's gardening web site. It is devoted to helping gardeners choose the best varieties for their region.) With all this to think about, don't try to depend on the garden for food security for the first few years. Enjoy it, learn from it, improve the quality of your diet, and save on grocery bills. Eventually, you'll be pleased by how much the garden can contribute.

Those of you who are avid gardeners can make a commitment to learn more. Permaculture and forest farming are worth exploring. The basic premise of permaculture is that it's as easy to plant a perennial plant (like a walnut tree or hazel nut shrub) as it is to plant an annual (such as a tomato or pepper). However, the perennial will produce far more food over far more years. Forest farming advocates encourage reforestation using food bearing plants. They also manage existing woodlands and forests to increase the food produced.

Even if you don't have a yard, you can try growing trees from seed. Avocados, most citrus, apples and pears, stone fruit such as peaches and plums all contain seeds that will grow. Raw whole nuts, still in their shells, can be planted too. While it is true that the fruit and nuts from seedlings don't always resemble their parent, don't let that stop you. Sometimes the seedling turns out to be an improvement. Even if yours don't, the trees will still make nice porch or patio plants and they will absorb carbon and produce oxygen throughout their lives. As the seedlings outgrow their pots and are ready to plant in the ground, seek permission to plant them around the perimeter of the community garden, a local park, or in a neighbor's, friend's, or relative's yard. Planting fruit and nut trees is an act of hope, a commitment to life.

Diversity has always been important in the garden. With the challenges of climate change, the need for diversity is dire. Make a commitment to growing a new food each season. The ones your family enjoys can be incorporated into future gardens. Food no one will eat makes good mulch or compost pile additions. As long as you are trying new things and reading about sustainable organic gardening, your food security will grow each season.

Gardening magazines can help you stay in touch with the sustainable gardening movement, whether you are a novice or adept gardener. Look for *The Mother Earth News*, *Organic Gardening*, and *Countryside Magazine*. You can also learn more by seeking out books, web sites, clubs, and associations devoted to the art of gardening. Classes are often offered through park and recreation departments and college extension programs. If you have trouble finding resources, ask for recommendations at the local library or bookstore, or from friends, family, or neighbors who garden. Most gardeners are happy to share information.

Be sure to check out Chapter 27, **More Resources**. Every section has listings that will enrich your gardening experience. (I also plan to finish the gardening book that this book interrupted. *Look for One Day at a Time in the Garden* through your favorite book store or library by the end of 2010.) Organic gardening can save the world. Why not get started right now?

Once you get your garden going, you are bound to have more produce than you can eat as it gets ripe. **Old Time Food Preservation and Storage**, the subject of our next chapter, will help you track down the information you need to store your produce for the winter season.

20. Old Time Food Preservation and Storage

Get more benefit from your garden with some old fashioned strategies to help food stay fresh longer. Root cellars and spring houses were our ancestors answer to keeping foods cool. For longer storage, and sometimes just for the jolt of flavor offered, foods were either fermented or dried. Below you will find a little more information on these resources and procedures.

Root Cellars are used to store various foods in areas that are not prone to soggy soil and flooding. They can be located under the house, or a short distance away. These underground rooms are cool year around and they are protected from extreme temperature fluctuations, which help keep food from spoiling. While they cannot compete with a refrigerator for keeping perishable foods fresh, they can maximize the shelf life of foods that are safe to store at room temperature—like potatoes and other roots, cabbage, winter squash, pumpkins, and home canned and dried foods. Before digging a root cellar, see the "Old Timers' Page" listed in the ***On the Web*** section of Chapter 27, **More Resources**.

Spring Houses were once used in a similar fashion to root cellars. They provide a place to keep food cool. A small building was erected over a stream or spring, and the cool water helped keep the temperature down. Special baskets or troughs were sometimes kept in the flowing water to cool down beverages, butter, and other perishables. *Foxfire 4* has information on spring houses and a whole lot more. The book may be in your library system and it is available from on-line book retailers. The entire *Foxfire Series* is very informative for those interested in living in harmony with the land.

Fermentation is used to make storable and tasty foods, such as sauerkraut and pickles. Proponents claim the food is more nutritious and more energy efficient than most other storage options. If you enjoy fermented food, you will want to check out the following web site: <http://www.extension.umn.edu/distribution/nutrition/DJ1091.html>. It discusses safety, flavor, and other things you need to know:

Drying and Dehydrating was once the main method of food preservation. In some areas slices of various foods were pierced and strung on cord and hung from the rafters, in a smoke house, in the branches of trees, or over the wood stove. Today, you can find all kinds of products, and plans, for a large number of devices for drying summer's bounty. Look into recommended temperatures and air flow when designing and building a sustainable system. Before you spend lots of money, experiment with low cost, low tech solutions. You will find more information than you can possibly use, by searching on "food drying" on the "Mother Earth News" web site: <http://www.motherearthnews.com/>

More Information: *Preserving Food Without Freezing or Canning* takes a novel approach to keeping produce fresh. The editors and authors focus on methods that discourage bacteria rather than destroying it. They have collected a large number of traditional recipes, from the French countryside, which use low or no heat and preserve vitamins and enzymes. Drying, fermentation, and preserving with salt and vinegar are some of the methods covered. Most of the recipes require storage temperatures to be between 50 and 56 degrees, which is most practical for folks who have root cellars or spring houses. *Preserving Food Without Freezing or Canning* is published by Chelsea Green. Libraries and bookstores can request a copy for you, and it is available from many on-line book sellers.

Next we are going to take a look at the basics for life in the Green World, oxygen and water, and our responsibilities to ensure their abundance and quality into the future.

21. Gram, The Green World, Oxygen & Water

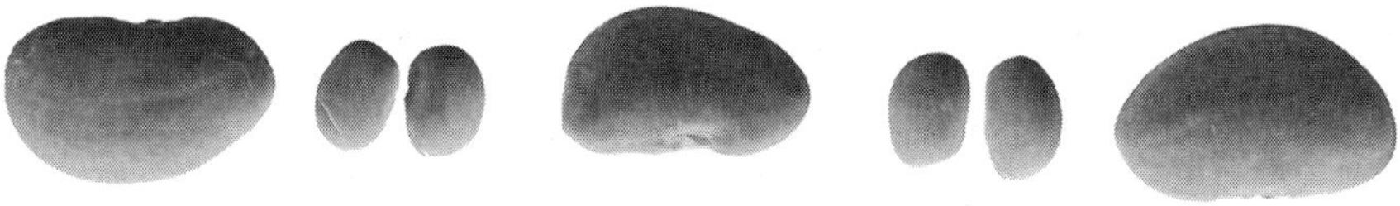

My grandmother believed in a peaceful green future. The world she taught me to yearn towards is similar to North America, six hundred years ago. In her vision the future would be a world without corner stores, shopping malls, mail order, or freeways. Gram said that it was important to think through how we would live. She believed we needed to learn certain old fashioned and traditional skills that would make life in that world easier and richer. She encouraged me to think about what plants would be useful, and to keep them growing near me.

Today, there are many people preaching the fall of western civilization. Some believe peak oil will cause a major crash. Others believe that the exhaustion of resources, such as metals, top soil, and clean water, will topple the corporate empires. A few believe we will eat ourselves out of house and home, and then simply starve to death. Last but not least, there are those who predict that global warming will change the environment in fundamental ways and that the earth will no longer support life. I am not sure what to think about any of this. I do know that we cannot continue unsustainable lifestyles and business without dire consequences. We must embrace the idea of living in the Green World, whether it is forced on us by the fall of modern civilization, or if we choose green in a more proactive way.

Today is a good time to think about the future. What skills do you want to pass down to your descendants to improve the quality of their lives? What skills do you want to learn, simply to survive, to thrive, no matter what the world looks like ten years from now? Which plants, for food, medicine, and utility do you want to have near you, as the world begins to change? Now is the time to brainstorm, research, and prepare.

Before we go on to **Useful Skills**, I want encourage you to think about two essential we often over look, and that we will definitely need in the Green World—oxygen and water. I am sure that Gram would agree, it is up to us to preserve them for today and for future generations.

Oxygen: We know we can't live without it; yet, very few of us think we have any responsibility to provide for our own oxygen needs. Six hundred years ago, much of North America was covered with thick woods, forests, and perennial grasslands. These oxygen producing environments spread over hundreds (and in some regions thousands) of miles in every direction. Now that we have cut most of our timber and plowed and paved our grasslands, we seem to feel that our ability to breathe is the responsibility of third world countries. They, on the other hand, are busy cutting down their trees for lumber, charcoal, and to make room for agriculture and other development. Logic seems to dictate that we reforest our own back yards, neighborhoods, parks, and open space. After all, no matter what kind of world we live in, we all need to breathe.

The Arbor Day Foundation is dedicated to greening our countryside and cities. They have a very informative web site,<http://www.arborday.org/> and you can join the foundation and receive ten free seedling trees to get started on your tree planting efforts.

When you are ready to participate in reforestation in a larger way, look into the Million Tree Project. Several municipalities and a handful of businesses have organized efforts to plant a million trees.

You can read about some of these projects on-line, and find out how you can help in these efforts:
Midwest US - <http://www.livinglandsandwaters.org/milliontrees/default.htm >
Southern CA - <http://www.milliontreesla.org/>
New York City - <http://www.milliontreesnyc.org/>

Water: Water issues were introduced in Chapter 6, **Location, Location, Location**, and Chapter 10, **Balance is Everything**; however, water is not only a location and storage issue. Having plenty of water available is a good start. Knowing how to utilize it and care for it is just as important. Ancient people depended on hand dug wells, spring boxes, small scale water catchment, and diversions built from bamboo, clay, slab wood, and rock. Look into local history, through books and museums, to find out how water was utilized in your area.

The modern world also offers appropriate solutions. There are low labor ways to improve springs and dig wells, for the right locations. Rain barrels and cisterns are good research subjects to assign to someone in your family or community. They can be put to use quickly and they can enhance property value. It is totally amazing how much water can be collected from the roofs of our dwellings and other structures. Near the end of this chapter you will find a list of web sites with information on utilizing and developing water resources. Also check the ***Recommended Reading*** section of Chapter 27, **More Resources,** where you will find a listing for *Holistic Management*. It has many chapters devoted to improving water cycles and water efficiency.

People who own, or are in the market to buy a piece of rural property, should take steps to assess the water quality on that land. It's important to understand how land use impacts water quality. The Virginia Cooperative Extension has a web site that will take you through the steps of a well thought out water assessment: <http://www.ext.vt.edu/pubs/farmasyst/442-915/442-915.html>

Water quality is a huge issue facing all of us today. The chemicals and agricultural run-off with which we currently contaminate our water will haunt us for many years. Don't think that corporations are the only ones to blame. Everything we use as a cleaner, in the laundry, flush down the toilet, pour down the drain, and use on the lawn, landscape, or garden—ends up in our water. The heavy elements and chemicals sink deep into aquifers and travel underground for hundreds, or even thousands, of miles before they come to the surface where they pollute wells and springs. The lightweight volatile elements and chemicals evaporate and accumulate in the atmosphere to fall with the rain on landscapes and natural areas both near and far. These chemicals are showing up in our water sheds and mountains, where they adversely affect our food chain and contaminate our drinking and agricultural water.

Take responsibility and go green at home. Buying (and growing) organic foods and using natural products contributes to the solution. Large scale commercial agriculture contaminates water with bacteria from large manure piles and lagoons and with agricultural chemicals. Pharmaceutical companies also contribute to the problem, both on the manufacturing end, and in the by-products we excrete after ingesting their products. Considering this pollution, it's a good idea to filter drinking water, and probably will be, for the next 1,000 years—at least.

A few web sites on home-made water filters are listed on the following page. For sustainability, design something using homemade ceramic components, and then incorporate clay, charcoal, or whatever your research and your region provide. For the short term, having camp or backpacking water filters in emergency caches is a good idea, but they won't last forever.

Water filtering On-Line:

Water filters can be made simply enough, here is a web site with a design that uses carbon: <http://www.baproducts.com/rainwatr.htm>

This web site shows **how to make charcoal**—the carbon portion in the filter above: <http://www.buyactivatedcharcoal.com/making_charcoal>

Here is **another filter design**. It uses clay soil instead of carbon: <http://www.parowanprophet.com/Nuclear_War_Comes/water_filter_instructions.htm>

Water Development On-Line:

Permaculture and Keyline water design use berms and swells to optimize water cycles: <http://www.foodnotlawns.com/keyline_water.html>

Rainwater catchment, rain barrels and cisterns: <http://solaralberta.ca/TUTORIAL/RAINCACH.HTM > (Be sure to check out the links at the bottom of the article. A little brainstorming on this topic may lead to designs built from slab wood, ceramic, cement, or rock.)

Hand dug wells:
<http://www.minifarmhomestead.com/homestead/wells.htm>

Spring development:
<http://www.or.nrcs.usda.gov/technical/conservation-planning-and-conservation-records/springdevelopment.html> (Sorry for the long web address. It has the best information I could find.)

Next, a plethora of Useful Skills will be outlined. Think of this as a family or community adventure. Each person can learn a new skill that will contribute to the sustainability of the group.

22. Useful Skills

My grandmother spent the last years of her life teaching me many skills that are unnecessary for life in the modern world. These skills have given me a very strong sense of stability and pleasure. Home canned soup, made from the products of my garden and my son's hunting and mushroom gathering, clarified fat, dried wild mushrooms, fruit preserves from wild and home grown trees and brambles, and an assortment of pickles—line my pantry shelves. I know how to cook on hot rocks, how to prepare acorn and wild seeds, which trees provide edible inner bark for lean times, and so much more. Grandmother was also keen on medicinal plants and that knowledge has served me well throughout my life. Even though these skills are not necessary for modern life, they enrich and improve that life. Passing them on will ensure resilience and flexibility to future generations.

The skills Gram taught me are good starting places for anyone wanting to live a more sustainable life. There are other skills you may want to look into, which will improve your ability to thrive in the days ahead. It would take many years for one individual to learn everything. However, we can each begin where we are and choose appropriate partners and collaborators to fill in the gaps. You can start by talking about disaster preparedness plans with family, neighbors, and friends. They might be willing to brainstorm and participate in planning and preparedness. Once you have some folks on the page with you, and good basic disaster plans, you can start proposing some ideas about skills the group may want to pursue.

If no one in your personal circle is interested, a good way to connect with like-minded people is in classes on wild foods, wild herbs, primitive skills, or survival skills. Check the class schedules of park and recreation centers, community colleges and universities, and science and history museums. Many newspapers and magazines also have calendars of upcoming events. Also look for alternative newspapers and magazines; they often have a wealth of opportunities. Check out the ***Educational Opportunities*** section of Chapter 27, **More Resources**. A number of organizations that offer classes are listed.

Introduce yourself to the folks you meet in these classes and suggest exchanging e-mail addresses or phone numbers. You might want to start a Yahoo group where you can stay in touch and exchange ideas. (Yahoo groups are free and easy to use: <http://groups.yahoo.com/>) If the computer is not your thing, you could suggest getting together at a local coffee shop or library to exchange ideas, share plans, and support each other towards a sustainable future. It may take awhile to put together a group that really clicks. When you do, each person could pursue different skills. Together you will be stronger and more prepared.

Beginning on the next page, you will find a list of skills appropriate for the Green World. Pick and choose what appeals to you, add some of your own ideas, and then prioritize according to need. For instance, those who live in very cold areas where freezing is an issue, may feel that fire making is essential. In areas that don't have surface water year around, water witching or dousing could be more important.

Basket Weaving utilizes plant material to make containers, mats, sandals, and many other items. There is a small industry that supplies prepared material for weavers. Purchased material is fine for those who are new learners; eventually, you will want to seek classes or workshops that cover gathering and preparing supplies directly from living plants. Look for weaving demonstrations offered through a local basket weavers or fiber arts guild, through local museums and farmers markets, or at regional arts and crafts shows. If you are unable to find a teacher or demonstrator locally, Miwok Archeological Preserve of Marin offers classes. You will find their contact information under ***Educational Opportunities*** in Chapter 27, **More Resources.**

Books on basket weaving are plentiful; however, it really helps to watch a demonstration—to better understand what the book is trying to convey. One very good book is *Cedar*; it has great graphics that show how to prepare and use weaving material from roots, bark, and shoots of the cedar tree. Many of these techniques could also be used for other plant materials. More information on *Cedar* is in the ***Recommended Reading*** section of Chapter 27, **More Resources**.

Bee Keeping: Honey and bees wax are not the only reasons to keep bees. They also produce other healthful substances, including bee pollen and royal jelly, and they help ensure good pollination rates for our garden, cane, bramble, and tree crops. Many communities have shops that offer bee keeping supplies, books, and even classes. Sometimes farm and garden centers also stock supplies and books. Wikipedia's "Bee Keeping" page is excellent, you can find it here: <http://en.wikipedia.org/wiki/Beekeeping>

Birth Control is important to quality of life, environmental health, and so much more. Most of the major problems facing mankind and the planet could have been avoided through adequate birth control. There are many sustainable alternative ways to reduce unplanned pregnancies. Some may not be as effective as modern birth control, but many are safer.

If you are of child bearing age, look into the alternatives suggested below; in case one day, the corner drug store no longer has what you need.

There are a number of modern low-tech, natural, family-planning techniques that are very safe, and when practiced carefully, are as effective as most other forms of birth control. They involve women paying close attention to their cycle and understanding when they are fertile. You can learn more on the Institute for Reproductive Health's web site: <http://www.irh.org/nfp.htm>

Herbal birth control is another option. Here is a short list of herbs used around the world: blue and black cohosh, pennyroyal, wild yam, papaya seed, and apricot pits. I have used some of these herbs myself and I know women that have used the others. Be sure to research the side effects and contra-indications and to find information on how to prepare and use the herbs, if you choose to do so. (The information on ***Herb Safety*** near the end of Chapter 14, **Other Essential Herbs**, will help your research efforts.) Indigenous birth control methods might make a good research topic, as well as what your ancestors did. Of course, some of our ancestors had ten or more children for generation after generation. We now know that this is not the wisest course.

Canning & Dehydrating: Home canning and dehydrating are great ways to stock up on high quality food. Growing a garden, buying by the box from the farmers market, or belonging to a CSA are good ways to get produce for home processing. (More information on Farmers Markets and CSA's are found in Chapter 5, **Food Security 101**.) While there are many books on canning and dehydrating, you will want to follow the guidelines set out by the National Center for Home Food Preservation. This will help you prevent food from becoming contaminated with organisms that cause spoilage and disease. You can find them on the web: <http://www.uga.edu/nchfp/index.html>. Once at the web site, you can order their book, sign up for an on line course, browse recommendations, and find recipes.

If you are not already set up with a canner and canning supplies, look into solar dehydrating instead. Once you are set up with a solar dryer, jars, lids, and reusable desiccant packages, there is nothing else to buy. Canning requires new lids every time you reuse a jar and new seals for the canner nearly every year, and canners are getting to be very pricey. You will find a source for more information in the section on ***Drying and Dehydrating*** in Chapter 20, **Old Time Food Preservation and Storage.**

Composting provides a way to turn food scraps, clothing made from natural fibers, paper products, cardboard, as well as garden and yard wastes into natural fertilizer for your garden. Look for classes and workshops through college extension programs and park and recreation departments. There are many books and web sites that discuss composting. My favorite is, *The Complete Compost Gardening Guide*, by Barbara Pleasant & Deborah L. Martin. They have composting plans and instructions that ought to work for every gardener—whether you have a tiny yard or a garden that spans several acres.

Cordage: Indigenous people made twine, string, and rope out of many different plant materials. Cattails, bulrushes, the bark from sage brush, wild iris leaves, and the inner bark from a number of different trees, are some examples. Cordage classes and demonstrations are occasionally available through museums, living history programs, university extension classes, and primitive skills schools. *Cedar*, listed under ***Recommended Reading*** in Chapter 27, **More Resources**, covers a variety of techniques for making cordage, twine, and rope. These techniques will work with many types of plant material, including bulrush and cattail.

Fire Making: Most of us have depended on matches our entire lives; however, matches are made using potassium, a nonrenewable resource. World supplies of potassium are dwindling. In many places matches are getting more expensive and in some areas of the world they are already scarce. The good news is that fire can be made using easy to find supplies. Fire making demonstrations are often offered during living history days and other similar events. Contact local history or Indian museums and ask about any up-coming demonstrations. When you attend a demonstration, be sure to take notes on the types of wood and other materials used, as well as the technique. Ask the person demonstrating if they have a business card. That way, after you have a chance to do some experimenting, you can find out about future demonstrations or sign up for a class. If you don't find any fire makers locally, the Miwok Archeological Preserve of Marin offers classes. Fire making is also covered in Tom Brown Jr.'s "Standard" course. You will find listings for both organizations in the ***Educational Opportunities*** section of Chapter 27, **More Resources**.

Gourd Growing and Crafting: Gourds are used to make bowls, spoons, canteens, water bottles, ladles, and many other useful objects. You need a long warm growing season and a reliable source of water to grow gourds. For the right location—gourds are an ideal renewable resource. Contact the American Gourd Society for more information: <http://www.americangourdsociety.org/ >. Click on the link to "Chapters," found right under the mast head, they may have meetings in your area. You will also find a link to "Publications" under the mast head. On the publications page, scroll down to find information on joining the Gourd Society. They publish a newsletter for members only, which is a good way to find seeds and get growing and crafting tips.

Hide Tanning can be learned from books, videos, home tanners, and primitive skills schools. This almost lost art will come in handy for anyone who raises meat animals or who hunts, should the corporate world cease to provide us with all our needs. *Deerskins into Buckskins: How To Tan With Natural Materials, a Field Guide for Hunters and Gatherers* by Matt Richards, Backcountry Publishing, 2004, is just one example of the many titles available through books stores and libraries.

Primitive Ceramics: You can learn how to find, dig, and process clay, and how to fire it in a pit or a hand built kiln. Many utilitarian and decorative objects can be made using the earth and the labor of your own hands. Ceramics, or pottery as it is often called, is very useful for folks who have limited access to carving wood or too short a growing season for gourds. There are many books on these processes; and some colleges, art centers, and primitive skills schools offer classes. One book you might enjoy is *How to Make Primitive Pottery,* by Evard H. Gibby, Eagles View Publishing, 1994. It describes how to find clay, processes it, fire it without a kiln, and then use your own earthen ware pot to cook a meal.

Seed Saving is best learned from an experienced seed saving gardener. A patient gardener can easily determine what you know about the birds and bees—when it comes to plant pollination and reproduction, and get you up to speed by showing you how it's all at work in the garden. Most gardeners are happy to share what they know. In fact, as I was writing this a young woman interrupted me to visit the garden. After showing her around, I sent her on her way with three potted plants, lots of seeds, and a few cuttings. She got a lesson in seed development, and she now knows when to come back to get some seed from some of the other plants she covets. Let any gardener know how much you appreciate their garden and they are very likely to reward you.

A great web site for beginners (and experienced gardeners and seed savers) is *The Seed Site*: <http://www.theseedsite.co.uk/>. You will find pages devoted to learning how to save seeds, germinate seeds, and how to recognize various seedlings when they have sprouted. It is the next best thing to having a gardening mentor.

Soap making classes are easy to find. However, what you really want to learn is sustainable soap making; that is to say, soap making that doesn't require you to purchase any supplies. Read class descriptions carefully. You may want to contact the instructor to clarify a few points. Many soap making classes revolve around purchased soap that you grate and melt and then add scent, dye, and other ingredients for custom bars or liquids. This sort of class will not contribute to sustainable soap making.

There are two different kinds of sustainable soap making. The first involves making soap from lye and vegetable oil or animal fat. While you can find books with instructions, I strongly recommend taking a class or working with an experienced person. Eventually you will need to learn how to make your own lye. For those who learn easily by following instructions, they can be found here: <http://www.wikihow.com/Make-Lye>. Making bar soap from homemade lye requires an additional step. You will need to find a copy of *Ben Franklin's Almanac of Wit, Wisdom, and Practical Advice: Useful Tips and Fascinating Facts for Every Day of the Year*, by the Editors of The Old Farmer's Almanac, Yankee Books, 2003. (It's available on Amazon.com.) In the entry for October 16, it briefly describes how to make both soft and hard soap from homemade lye. However, it doesn't give exact amounts or tell you where to find supplies, so it may take a little experimenting to get it right. (You will also need a sustainable, on-going source of oil or fat. See Chapter 11, **Process Your Own Fats and Oils**.)

The other type of soap making uses plant material that is high in saponins. It is much rarer to find instruction in plant saponin based soap making, although many indigenous people completely relied on this type of soap for all their cleaning needs. If you are a fan of herbs and herb books, you will occasionally come across references to plants like Ceanothus and bouncing-bet being used for soap. My personal best results came from soap lily; however these plants are fairly rare and take a long time to grow. This is a subject that needs some diligent research and experimentation, but for those who love all things herbal, it will be lots of fun.

Spinning, Weaving, Crochet, and Knitting are often thought of as the process of turning animal hair or wool into clothing and other utilitarian or artistic materials. Some plant fibers, such as cotton and flax can also be spun. If you live in a cold winter area, wool is really the best bet. Where hot weather is the challenge, look into growing and spinning plant fibers. Spinners and weavers guilds are wide spread; they will help you find teachers and initial supplies. Search on the Internet, ask the local chamber of commerce or visitors' center, and visit local county and craft fairs, and farmers markets. Spinning guild members often display their creations or give demonstrations at these events. You can also get an idea about what's involved by requesting *The Art of the Loom, Weaving, Spinning & Dyeing Across the World*, from the local library. It is by Ann Hecht, University of Washington Press. If they don't have this exact title, they are sure to have something similar.

Traditional and Alternative Building includes stone masonry, cob, straw bale construction, log, and cord wood building. Yestermorrow Design/Build School is one source of training. <http://www.yestermorrow.org/ > Also check the ***Educational Opportunities*** section of Chapter 27, **More Resources**. Several of the listings offer sustainable building courses.

Traditional Farming techniques are not always sustainable in the modern world, but they are worth looking into. Discovering what indigenous people and pioneers grew for food, and what techniques they used, can point you in the direction of sustainable options. Slash and burn (where forests and savannahs were cut down and burned to make way for crops), for instance, was sustainable when there were very few people and lots of land. It is devastating to our environment today. So, while you use the library, the Internet, and local historical societies to research traditional farming techniques, also look for information on organic and sustainable farming. A hybrid between traditional and modern practices might just work perfectly. The most important thing is to seek sustainable techniques that are adapted to your region.

Traditional Food Preservation generally focuses on drying and storing a variety of staples and seasonings. Seek information on techniques used historically by local indigenous people, or those used by your ancestors.

Visit local museums and history centers to find out what sorts of food folks saved in the past. Talk to the elders or "old timers" in your family or community, who may have stories about food preservation from their childhoods. Many books are available through public and university libraries. There may be a living history group associated with a local mission, fort, or museum. Joining a living history group is a good way to learn many traditional skills. Learning about traditional food preservation is best done with a mentor; however, there is a great book out: *Preserving Food without Freezing or Canning, Traditional Techniques Using Salt, Oil, Alcohol, Vinegar, Drying, Cold Storage and Lactic Fermentation*, from Chelsea Green Publishing Company. Also see Chapter 20, **Old Time Food Preservation and Storage**.

Traditional & Primitive Tool Making including ***Flint Knapping and Bow and Arrow Construction*** opportunities are sometimes found through museum demonstrations or living history days. Primitive skills schools are another source of information. Check with the local chamber of commerce, they may know about primitive skills schools in your area. You can also use your favorite search engine to find schools, centers, and other organizations under "Primitive Skills." Also try searching on "Mountain Man Rendezvous." These fun events often feature living history demonstrations, competitions, and displays where you can connect with those who offer appropriate classes, books, and instructional videos. If you don't find any tool makers locally, the Miwok Archeological Preserve of Marin offers classes. Tool making is also introduced in Tom Brown Jr.'s "Standard" course, and covered in more detail in advanced classes. You will find listings for both organizations in the ***Educational Opportunities*** section of Chapter 27, **More Resources**.

Vinegar Making: Diluted vinegar makes a great cleaning fluid, facial astringent, hair rinse, flavoring for salad dressings, preservative for pickles, and some folks even add a little to their morning juice for its medicinal properties. Here's a web site that will help you get started on vinegar making: <http://www.vinegarman.com/VinegarMaking.shtml>

Water Witching or Dousing is the art of finding underground springs, streams, and other water sources. In the old days every community had at least one water witch or dowser. Typically the dowser holds a forked stick, or a pendulum, and walks the property in question until they find the area with the strongest "pull." Dousing is not hard to learn, if you have the latent talent. Finding a reliable dowser to teach you is the hardest part. Ask local well drilling companies for recommendations. They ought to know who has the gift and who doesn't. Next, contact the dowser and ask if they teach classes or offer demonstrations. Young, hardy, and hale dowsers might not be eager to train their competition. If this is the case, make use of their services, befriend them the best you can, and when the time comes you can hope you're chosen to follow in their footsteps.

Waste Management: Disasters can interfere with the proper functioning of sewer lines and septic systems. Having a back up waste management plan is a good idea, even for those who are happy with their current systems. (It wouldn't hurt any of us to think about managing our personal waste more sustainably.) Get informed about out-houses, pit toilets, saw dust toilets, and composting toilets. High tech and do it yourself solutions are available. Read up on the subject and have the advantages and possible risks well in mind before you decide on a system. *The Humanure Handbook,* by Joseph Jenkins is one of the best books on the subject. It may be available by request through local libraries, and it is also available from Amazon.com.

Whittling and Wood Carving are useful for making cups, bowls, forks, combs, and replacement parts such as eye hooks, drawer pulls, and simple latches. Where trees are plentiful, the growing season too short for gourds, and where clay is rare—simple wood working skills can provide for many needs. Attend living history demonstrations and country fairs to find folks that whittle and carve. The book, *American Indian Survival Skills,* provides a good introduction; see the ***Recommended Reading*** section of Chapter 27, **More Resources**.

Wild Foods & Medicines: In addition to gardening and food storage, you may want to learn about wild foods and medicines. Wild plants are often more adaptable and hardy than those we grow in our gardens. Every few weeks I take note of all the wild food in the fields and vacant lots around me. At times, there is literally tons of food being ignored nearby. Depending on the area and the season, the same is true for many parts of the world. This food would take a bit of labor to process, but having the know-how will help you adapt as the climate changes. Some people feel that herbal medicine is not as effective as commercial medicines, but perhaps one day, either from choice or necessity, it will be the only kind we have. Seek classes on wild foods and medicines through herb stores, park and recreation centers, college extension programs, and alternative health centers. If classes aren't available in your area, see the listing for the California School for Herbal Medicine in the section on ***Educational Opportunities***, Chapter 27, **More Resources**. There are also many books on the subject, visit the local library or bookstore and ask for recommendations.

Once we have decided on a skill we would like to become adept at, it's time to get ready to be the student. We need to cultivate some specific qualities and attitudes to get the most out of the time we invest in learning. These qualities and attitudes are covered in our next chapter.

23. So You Want To Be An Apprentice?

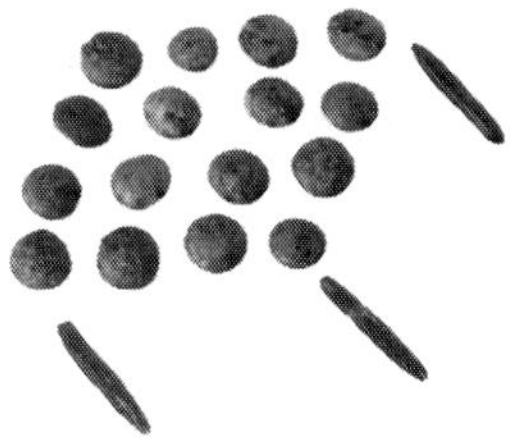

The best ways to learn sustainable skills is to find a knowledgeable person willing to take you under their wing. Books, magazines, web sites, and demonstrations will get you started, but to truly master a discipline of any kind, you need to spend time with a master.

That old saying, "when the student is ready, the teacher will appear," is right on target. To get ready to follow in the master's footsteps, you will need to cultivate patience, helpfulness, kindness, and flexibility. The master teacher may have very different political or religious views than you. A non-judgmental outlook and a little humility and humbleness will go far. You will also need the ability to put your ego on the back burner, which is much easier said than done.

Practicing at being the student (or the apprentice) is a valuable exercise. Perhaps you know someone who throws pots, cooks a mean apple pie, or has a bountiful garden. Ask them to teach you or offer to help them. Let them be the master while your ego takes the back seat. Absorb all you can. If you find yourself critiquing their style or wanting to prove your own knowledge, you might need to repeat this exercise a few times before you can gracefully take the subservient role. As difficult as this can be, it is necessary to absorb all the nuances of what a true master offers. However, keep in mind that we are talking about learning an art, a discipline, or a skill. We are not talking about this person demeaning you, involving themselves in your personal life, touching your body, or recruiting you for their "tribe," "clan," or anything else. Both the apprentice and the teacher need to set and maintain healthy boundaries.

Once you feel ready to be the apprentice, narrow the subjects you are interested in down to a few key skills. Seek related titles from well stocked magazine and book racks (the authors contact information, web site, or class schedule may be listed), look through the local newspapers' community calendar, add your contact information to local museums' and nature centers' mailing lists, visit craft and county fairs where there are often demonstrators, and/or search on-line for classes that interest you.

If you don't find classes locally, try contacting instructors from other areas. Many of the folks who teach classes on traditional and primitive skills maintain web sites, or have contact information posted on the web sites of organizations for which they teach. Ask if they would be available to teach in your area, and offer to act as a liaison. You can contact local sponsoring organizations, arrange lodging, meals, and/or transportation. This extra effort may make the difference between a "yes" and a "no." Once those arrangements are taken care of, the next step might be to help with planning or publicity. Planning and publicizing events is not difficult, but diligence and organization are necessary. Tips for beginners are available on-line: <http://groups.yahoo.com/group/ncanativeeventsandnews/> Click on "Files" from the navigation bar on the left, then look for the file named "Press Release Guru." (You may be prompted to join the group before you can access the files page.)

The rare individual who has great skills might not have the time or patience to take on anything new. As a beginner, your first teacher just needs to know a little more than you. Start off by apprenticing yourself to the apprentice. Practice your new skills, read all you can, and attend meetings or events on the subject. As you progress it is very likely that the master teacher will appear.

When you find a master teacher with time for you, let them know you value their skill, and offer value in exchange. Some teachers offer organized classes, demonstrations, or apprenticeship programs—and charge a set fee. Others don't see themselves as teachers; however, their time is worth as much as those with organized classes. If you get quality one on one instruction, the time they spend with you is very valuable. Offer to do what you can for them. Help them around the house or garden, cook them a nice meal, and/or share your specialized skills. (Perhaps you are a good mechanic or carpenter.) Find a way to make yourself useful and the relationship is likely to flourish.

Practice what you learn, polish your skills, and find opportunities to show your work to the teacher. Take criticism gracefully and ask questions when you are unsure how to proceed. Many skills evolve slowly; the teacher probably knows far more than you can learn in a few months or even a few years. Respect the relationship, as you become more skilled it may not be as close, but it is always wise to check back in with the teacher from time to time.

Most importantly, respect and honor the teacher's intellectual property. The knowledge they share with you belongs to them. Do not publish, record, sell, or offer formal classes without their permission. Always credit your source, and offer fair value to the teacher for any money or other tangibles you earn from the skills they have taught you. When we are honorable in our learning endeavors, it helps heal the fabric of our communities, and it ensures our readiness when the next teacher appears.

Speaking of teachers, the learning process is accelerated by teaching and demonstrating what you have learned. Through your learning and apprenticeships, ultimately, you are preparing to become a teacher yourself. Teaching, which deepens learning and life, is the subject of our next chapter.

24. Each One Teach One

Teaching, at least one other person, deepens our knowledge; whether we are new to a particular study or a long time practitioner. To teach, we must first bring awareness to what we do, focus on it, discern the many disciplines, break them down into steps, and think through how we will describe the processes. Then, when we work with a student, we must be attentive and mindful. To succeed, our descriptions and demonstrations must relay meaningful and useful information. If not, it is up to us, as teachers, to trouble shoot the process and find new ways to describe, depict, or demonstrate the necessary steps. What the teacher gains, in both tangible and intangible benefits, is at least as much as the student gains, especially in the early stages of teaching.

Students don't need to articulate the processes of, say, weaving a basket or identifying a plant, as learners. Once they engage in teaching another person, this articulation is necessary. Thinking through the process, and describing and demonstrating it to another person stimulates the kind of brain activity that leads to strong and accessible memories. Teaching, even when we are not sure of ourselves, helps us own what we are trying to learn. Learners can share with friends, family, neighbors, or community members. Perhaps you can form a partnership with someone who is learning a different skill. Then you can trade lessons, alternating between being the teacher and the student. When there are safety issues, double check your information and processes. Don't bluster through mushroom identification, for instance. Too much is at stake.

New learners aren't the only ones who benefit from teaching. Perhaps you have been canning, collecting wild berries, or making tools for decades and never considered that anyone would want to learn your skills. Your own children and grandchildren may ignore or look askance at your backwards "pastimes." However, there are others who would love to learn what you know. Your old fashioned skills are very valuable. Don't let them fade away.

You may find opportunities to share what you know through a master gardeners or master food preservers program (administered through the local county agricultural extension). Clubs, societies, and guilds are other great places to share. Look for living history associations through local and regional museums. If you produce something tangible, enter it in the local county fair or juried arts and crafts shows. Volunteering to demonstrate can also be very rewarding.

Make yourself available, share and network with others, and when you are ready, the student will appear. Your student might have wild colored hair, wear weird clothes, or have more things pieced than you want to know about. Instead of rejecting the accouterments of youth, culture, political affiliation, or religion—look for the sincerity and enthusiasm of your potential student. However, you also want to keep your wits about you and be safe. Until you are sure of the potential student's trust-worthiness, remember that they are an unknown quantity. Don't let their enthusiasm over ride your good sense. We need to set our own boundaries about who we invite into our homes, workshops, gardens, personal vehicles, and out into the woods. Revisit the classic movie, "Kung Fu," with David Carradine. David Carradine, as Kwai Chang Caine, apprenticed himself to Master Po. Master Po kept his emotions restrained in his relationship with his apprentice. This restraint is a good model for all of us, as we endeavor to keep our knowledge alive on the planet.

Teaching can have some small risk, but it is very rewarding. We grow through the process of teaching. It can bring us a sense of grace, a connection to the past, and to future generations. The enthusiasm the true student carries enriches us. What is simple and mundane in our own eyes begins to shine bright as jewels. As our students learn our craft, they often bring a new perspective, creativity, and a spirit of experimentation and adventure that we may have lost long ago. This new perspective can awaken our own creativity and passion, renewing our relationship with our craft.

As we develop our skills as teachers, the autumn years of our lives grow near. In the old days, elders exchanged wisdom and experience for assistance with tasks that once took little thought or effort. Don't underestimate the value of possible future exchanges of this kind. Perhaps one day you will need help bringing in the fire wood or threading a needle. By becoming a skilled teacher today, you pave the way for that exchange to happen tomorrow.

Modern life is alienating to everyone. Young and middle aged adults are kept so busy running a gauntlet between education, work, family, and networking activities that they don't have time for their elders. Those elders languish in care homes, unvalued and unvisited; or perhaps worse, they become a burden to families already over their limits. All is not right with our world. We need to envision the future as a different place, a Green World, where elders are valued and knowledge is shared. To ensure we can survive the transition, it is time to learn, to teach, and to share.

Part of this revisoning of the future needs to include our economic system and our careers, which is the subject of our next chapter.

25. Rethinking Economies and Careers

Our economy is changing, as it must. Production, storage, and transportation of goods and services rely on nonrenewable resources, which are now in short supply. We feel the effects in the current state of inflation, many goods and services have tripled in price over the last few years. Under this economic pressure, households must cut back on their spending to make ends meet. Production lags—as demand falls, corporations down size, people lose their jobs, and spending is further reduced.

Trying to prop up the old system cannot succeed. Together we must dream of a different system, where production depends on labor and the creativity of our hands and minds. Modern culture has taught us to balk at the idea of labor. Our current education system strives to erase the creative process from both adults and children. In exchange, we have epidemic rates of obesity, diabetes, high blood pressure, heart disease, stress related conditions, and chronic depression. We all know there has to be a better way.

Labor and creativity are necessary to human health, both mentally and physically. Corporations, who take the wealth of the many and concentrate it in the hands of a few, depend on you to believe otherwise. As long as you disdain labor and undervalue creativity, you are happy to spend your hard earned money on shoddy corporate goods and inferior processed foods, much to the detriment of your own health and the health of the planet that supports us. It is definitely time for a change.

Start with a garden. Your labor and creativity will combine to provide food for your family, flowers for pollinators, and habitat for birds and other beneficial creatures. Expand by learning to produce sustainable household products with the raw materials that nature provides. (Chapter 22, **Useful Skills**, will give you some great ideas.) Next, you can begin imagining a regional economy where human needs are provided through skill, labor, and creativity in combination with local renewable resources.

One of my neighbors provides a good example. Jeff Marshall raises horses, and is now training them to pull wagons. "As gas gets more expensive, people will still need to get around. I will be able to provide transportation, for people and goods, and heck, it will be a whole lot of fun too." Jeff has purchased a number of wagons and an old horse drawn carriage—the driver is protected from the elements, behind a windshield complete with wipers. He is also collecting books on building and repairing the wagons, as well as the harnesses for the horses. His excitement is contagious. I hope to be one of his first passengers.

You might think, "Well, that is fine for Jeff, but what about me?" Those who are less physically able may find that basket weaving, ceramics, knitting, or crocheting are more in the realm of doable vocations. Communities need many different skills to thrive. Everyone can find a place, whether it involves record keeping, tending or teaching children, keeping the crows out of the corn, or any of a multitude of tasks. Our current skills, those we choose to learn, our creativity, labor, and renewable resources will lead us to new economies and careers. Embrace this change with Jeff's enthusiasm. The Green World is going to be a creative, healthy, fun place.

26. Take Time to Reflect

A long time ago, when my grandmother was telling me stories about the Green World, she impressed on me how important it was to decide what we would take with us. I now understand that she didn't only mean the sort of things we pack in an emergency cache. While she made sure I thought about the food, utility, and medicine plants I would want to have with me, as well as the skills necessary to survive, there are other, perhaps more important things to consider.

Our ideals, beliefs, and experience will become the basis of the teachings that get handed down to our descendants. Many cultures hold that there were worlds before this one, and that there will be worlds after this one. These cultures pass teachings that tell how the earth was destroyed by unsustainable practices. They also have teachings that point the way to preserving earth's balance. We need to think carefully about engendering respect for the environments that support us and passing that respect far into the future. And we must begin practicing that respect today.

"Live simply, so others can simply live." I'm not sure where I first heard this quote. It now haunts me. As a young woman I didn't understand how what I did in the US could possibly cause harm in African villages or distant rain forests. Now I know better. The electricity I use is made from burning fossil fuels, which adds carbon to the air (and contributes to climate change and catastrophic weather). The demand I place on that fuel, through using electricity, causes the price to rise. Food prices and fuel prices are inextricably bound. I have been writing this book to you, Dear Reader, with the lights turned off and the clocks unplugged, hoping to hold back prices so that people in Haiti and Africa can afford to eat.

Live simply. Pray. Dream a story to carry all you have learned, all you will learn, to our descendants in the Green World.

27. More Resources

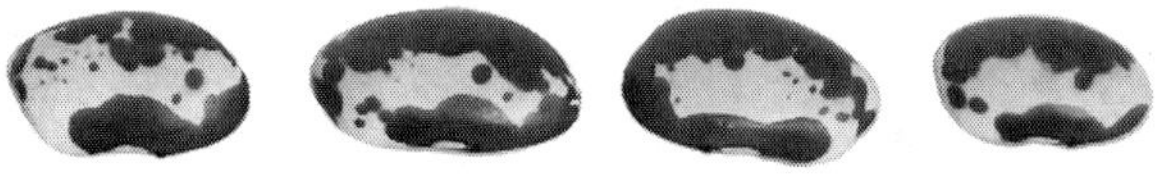

You will find many resources in the text of each chapter. Those that are mentioned more than once are found here, as well as some additional resources that will contribute to your knowledge of the subjects at hand. These resources are divided into the following sections: ***On the Web***, ***Recommended Reading***, ***Sources for Gardeners***, and ***Educational Opportunities***.

On the Web

Many libraries now have public Internet access computers, and some have helpful volunteers, orientations, or classes. When these services are not available, the librarian can probably direct you to a local organization that can help.

While the Internet is a great research tool, web sites sometimes evaporate into thin air for no apparent reason. If any of the Internet sites listed in this book aren't there when you need them, try searching on the topic to see what you can find. If you are not able to find the information you need, you might have to turn local libraries, bookstores, or an on-line bookseller. If you still are not successful, please send an e-mail to: bio-diversepress@ymail.com. Let them know what you are seeking. If they can find a web site or book that covers the information they will post it on their web site: <http://www.BioDiversePress.com>. If not, they will look for a knowledgeable person to cover the topic in a future book.

Below you will find a number of useful web sites to deepen your knowledge of the some of the subjects covered in this book.

Advocacy and Action:

"What you can do about fuel and food prices:" <http://harvestsgardeningsecrets.blogspot.com/2008/05/what-you-can-do-about-food-\fuel-prices.html> (It's simpler than you think!)

Gardening:

"When Food Prices Rise, Planting a Garden is Wise:" <http://groups.yahoo.com/group/ncanativeeventsandnews/message/10750> (Offers tips on what to grow in a food security garden.)

The Calorie Connection: <http://groups.yahoo.com/group/ncanativeeventsandnews/message/11058> (We normally look to our gardens to provide low cal foods, but with over five million agricultural acres taken out of production because of floods and droughts, growing your own calories is a good idea.)

Cornell University offers a web site for home gardeners to network and share information on the best vegetable varieties for various parts of the country. You can check it out at: <http://www.vegvariety.cce.cornell.edu>

Learn More:

This "Old Timer Page" contains links to information on a wealth of skills and ideas: <http://waltonfeed.com/old/index.html>

Jason Godesky's "Thirty Theses;" discusses the coming fall of Western Civilization. Each of the theses is linked to a thoughtful and thought provoking essay, which in turn are linked to references and documentation. <http://anthropik.com/thirty/>

"The Little Ice Age" article, from Wikipedia, helps us understand some of what we are up against in regards to climate change: <http://en.wikipedia.org/wiki/Little_Ice_Age>. You will also find links, in the article, to other historic episodes of climate change, famine, and plague.)

News:

Food, Fuel, and Economic Crises News:
<http://groups.yahoo.com/group/harvests_thoughts/>

News on Climate and Earth Changes can be found here:
<http://360.yahoo.com/harvest95546> (Look for the blog link.)

Recommended Reading:

American Indian Survival Skills; by W. Ben Hunt; Meredith Press, 1991. Fashioning handmade drills, knives and sheaths, spears, traps, shelter, furniture, sandals, kitchen ware, snowshoes, sleds, snow goggles, animal harnesses and packs are covered. Illustrated techniques for whittling, hand weaving, making rawhide, as well as bark and woven baskets are also included. If you have never cooked over a fire you will appreciate the suggestions for setting up cooking fires, frying pans, coffee pots, Dutch ovens, and spits. You'll be confidently cooking outdoors in no time at all.

Animal, Vegetable, Miracle; by Barbara Kingsolver; Harper Collins, 2007. Kingsolver shares her family's decision to leave the urban southwest for a more sustainable rural lifestyle. She, her husband, and their two daughters spend a year eating locally produced food. They garden, keep chickens and turkeys, make cheese, store food for winter, and shop the local farmers market—all in gourmet and highly sociable style! You will find tips, recipes, and inspiration for living sustainably while entertaining friends and nurturing family.

Cedar; by Hilary Stewart; University of Washington Press, 1984. This sumptuously illustrated book covers cordage, basket weaving, building boats and plank houses, traditional cooking, bent wood containers, as well as lots of information on the indigenous cultures of the Pacific Northwest.

The Complete Compost Gardening Guide; by Barbara Pleasant & Deborah L. Martin; Story Publishing, 2008. Everything you need to know about making and using compost can be found in the pages of this easy to understand book. Whether your garden is large or small, and whether you have a lot of time or very little, you will find a plan that will work for you.

Designing and Maintaining Your Edible Landscape – Naturally; by Robert Kourik; Metamorphic Press, 1986. Rather than focusing on a single philosophy, Kourik provides a fairly in depth analysis of many popular organic practices. By comparing their strong and weak points, he helps the average (yet intellectual) gardener decide what may work best for their situation and inclination. This book will help you sort fact from myth.

Gardening Without Work, For the Aging, the Busy, and the Indolent; by Ruth Stout; Lyons Press, 1998. Ruth Stout has been writing about organic gardening since 1955! She inspired many of us to use mulch, which reduces work and improves soil. Her easy to follow plans will point you in the right direction, even if you have never held a seed packet or a garden trowel.

Holistic Management, A New Framework for Decision Making; by Allen Savory; Island Press; 1999. Everyone who has an interest in a sustainable future for our planet will find Holistic Management very informative. Many long held land management beliefs have been proven detrimental to our ecosystems. Read this and know the facts.

In Defense of Food, an Eater's Manifesto; by Michael Pollan; Penguin Press, 2008. This book takes a good look at the Western diet and urges us to eat real food instead of the industrial and unhealthy products that commonly pass for food. Michael Pollan outlines a sustainable diet that would suit itself to gardening and storing unprocessed staples.

Joy of Cooking; by Irma S. Rombauer and Marion Rombauer Becker; Plume, 1975. This old fashioned cook book has directions for preparing everything you hunt, slaughter, or grow; including skinning a rabbit, cooking game, shell fish, and all sorts of animal parts you might otherwise throw away. Canning, preserving, brining, and pickling are well covered. There are tons of recipes, both everyday and extra fancy, for everything your garden, farm, field, or forest is likely to produce. Also featured are a number of recipes for dry beans, and instructions on growing sprouts from many types of grain and seed.

Nutrition Secrets of the Ancients, Foods and Recipes for Optimum Health; by Dr. Gene Spiller and Rowena Hubbard; Prima Publishing, 1996. If you want to know about the most nutritious foods for storage and gardening, this book has the answers. Foods from many cultures are included, with preparation tips and recipes. Many recipes feature dry beans or whole grains and garden fresh produce. Especially noteworthy, amaranth and quinoa are covered. These grains are easily grown in the back yard. This book is currently out of print, but it is still available through libraries and used book outlets. It is definitely worth seeking out.

Tom Brown's Field Guide to Wilderness Survival; published by Berkley Trade, 1987. Learn how to build natural shelters in plains, woods, or deserts; find safe drinking water; make fire without matches; find, stalk, kill, and prepare animals for food; and much more. Tom Brown has a number of other useful titles in print. You can find all of his books on his web site: <http://www.trackerschool.com/> (Choose "Tracker Store" from the navigation links under the masthead, and then books. You can also use the search function once you reach the store to find specific topics of interest.)

You Can Farm; by Joel Salatin; Polyface, 1998. Dreaming of a sustainable farm for self sufficiency or profit? Salatin shows you the ropes, from how to get started even if you don't have land, how to care for land sustainably, how to market what you grow, and how to make a profit. Experienced farmers will also appreciate his ideas about land management and diversity—both for sustainability and profit. (He is all about making a profit.) Keep a notebook handy as you read; he makes lots of recommendations on other authors and books.

Whole Grains, Grow, Harvest & Cook Your Own; by Sara Pitzer; Garden Way Publishing, 1981. If you are ready to start experimenting with growing or cooking whole grains, this book will point the way. It is now out of print, but still available at reasonable prices, and there doesn't seem to be anything comparable in print. Ask your librarian, favorite used book store, or check with on-line book sellers.

Sources for Gardeners:

Bountiful Gardens seed catalog is a must have for folks turning to organic gardening for the first time. The catalog offers many unusual varieties, as well as information on "a sustainable solution to growing food." 18001 Shafer Ranch Road, Willits CA 95490, (707) 459-6410, <http://www.bountifulgardens.org>

Forest Farm is the catalogue for tree planters! Over five hundred pages are devoted to trees, shrubs, vines, and perennials—many of them useful for habitat or food. They charge $5.00 for this hefty paperback book, but you can shop on line for free. 990 Tetherow Road, OR 97544-9599 <http://www.forestfarm.com>

Horizon Herbs carries a large number of medicinal herbs and unusual edibles as seeds and plants. P. O. Box 69, Williams, OR 97544-0069, (541) 846-6704 <http://www.horizonherbs.com>

J.L. Hudson, Seedsman will wow you with their selection. They offer varieties of edible plant seeds that you won't find anywhere else. For those interested in growing unusual tree crops from seeds, this is the place to get started. P.O. Box 337, La Honda, California 94020, <http://www.JL-HudsonSeeds.net>

Richter's herb catalog deserves a place on every aspiring herbalist's reference shelf, it is that informative. Their focus is medicinal plants and seeds. In addition, they carry a nice selection of vegetables, culinary herbs, and flowers. Located in Canada, you can request a catalog by phone: (905) 640-6677 or Fax: (905) 640-6641. <http://www.Richters.com>

Seed Savers Exchange focuses on heirloom, open pollinated vegetables. Their catalog will make you drool. They offer many unusual and tasty old time vegetables that will help you increase the diversity of your garden. 3094 North Winn Road, Decorah, Iowa 52101, <http://www.seedsavers.org>

Educational Opportunities:

California School of Herbal Studies provides a variety of short and long term classes; including herb walks, mushroom identification, and medicine making. The long term training is pricey, but the short term classes are reasonable. Limited lodging and camping can be found within a short drive. They are located at 9309 Highway 116, Forestville, California. Mailing address: PO Box 39, Forestville, CA 95436 Phone: (707) 887-7457; E-mail: cshs@cshs.com; and on the web at: <http://www.cshs.com/index.html>

Cob Cottage offers training in sustainable building, permaculture, rocket stoves and more. Classes are offered in Oregon and at various locations around the world. They also have videos and books available for those unable to attend classes. Contact them at: Cob Cottage Company, PO Box 942, Coquille, OR 97423, (541)396-1825, <http://www.cobcottage.com>

Indigenous Permaculture Program (IPP) is a grassroots organization advancing community food security, by sharing information, tools, and resources for traditional indigenous farming and appropriate technology. Their mission is to help re-establish wellness to Mother Earth and her people, and to enable Native and local low-income people to create sustainable communities. Contact Information: 3288 21st St. #192, San Francisco, CA 94110, 415-370-1657, <http://www.indigenous-permaculture.org>, ipp@ecologycenter.org

Miwok Archeological Preserve of Marin holds classes in traditional skills such as fire making, basketry, bow and arrow construction, and flint knapping. Classes are reasonably priced, there are no prerequisites, and camping options are plentiful. For more information contact the director, Sylvia Thalman, at 415 479-3281; by mail: MAPOM, PO Box 481, Novato CA 94948; by e-mail: sylthal@aol.com, or on the web: <http://www.mapom.org/index.htm>

Solar Energy International (SEI) is a non-profit organization whose mission is to help others use renewable energy and environmental building technologies through education. SEI teaches individuals from all walks of life how to design, install and maintain renewable energy systems, and how to design and build efficient, sustainable homes. SEI offers trainings online and in 22 locations around the world. PO Box 715, 76 S. 2nd St., Carbondale, CO 8162, 970-963-8855, fax: 970-963-8866, sei@solarenergy.org <http://www.solarenergy.org/>

Springs Preserve in Las Vegas offers a number of classes on wild foods, gardening, sustainable building, and ecological restoration. When you visit their web site, you will find the link to "Education" in tiny print at the bottom of the page. Click on "Adult Programs" and then choose "Sustainable Living," or "In the Garden" to view a selection of classes. Classes are very reasonable, and lodging and dinning opportunities abound. You can visit their web site at: <http://www.springspreserve.org/>. If you are close enough to stop by they are located at: 333 S. Valley View Blvd., Las Vegas, Nevada (between US 95 and Alta Drive). You can also contact them by Phone: (702) 822-7700 or by mail: P.O. Box 98947, Las Vegas, NV 89193

Tom Brown Jr.'s Tracker School offers training in a variety of sustainable practices. Tom Brown Jr. is the author of 14 books, which range in subject matter from philosophy to wild edible foods and medicines. His courses are pricey and most require that you take the "Standard" course as a prerequisite. However, that standard course covers an amazing amount of information. Visit: <http://www.trackerschool.com/> To find the course description, click on "Schedule," then "Full Schedule" for the appropriate year, scroll down the classes to "Standard" and click there, and then click on "Teaching" from the "Tracker Tree" on the left of the page.

About the Author

By Jessie Palmer

Harvest lives in a quaint quiet home at the end of a row of houses on the north end of the Hoopa Valley Indian Reservation. In the twelve years she has lived here, she has become the local expert in gardening. She is the "Auntie" to many young men and women who have found that Harvest is enthusiastic to share her knowledge and wisdom.

I came to know Harvest through a note I had left, which was a slightly unusual set of circumstances, involving an abandoned mother dog and puppies that she had been feeding. We had several conversations, both in person and over the phone, before I came to her house.

The first time I visited Harvest's home, the directions described it as the only house on the street with a garden. I was confused as I slowly drove down the street. The only garden appeared to be a maze of intensely inter cropped flowers, fruits and vegetables that seemingly belonged to no house. It was a busy metropolis of bees, butterflies and other pollinators hard at work. As I approached closer, I began to see that there was a home behind the swarming array of flora and fauna. I never thought that her home and garden would be so graciously welcoming to me, that it would become the place for many adventures fall, winter, spring and summer.

Harvest is an inspiration. She has challenged me to rethink the role and order of a garden in one's life. Ignoring conventional gardening techniques, she does not till her soil in the spring, creating nice neat rows. Nor does she retire her garden in the late summer or fall. Instead gardening is a way of life; it's a season to season cycle of living all year round. Her daily routine begins by gathering a days or meals worth of fresh from the garden produce. She cooks her meals with unprocessed staples and treats such as edible flowers, berries and hearty squash. What is not used is returned to the ground. The very sweepings from the floor and hairs from her head are food and replenishment to the creatures that work hard to maintain a healthy soil life.

Fall is a welcomed transition. Long smoldering hot summer days slowly fade into the shorter cooler days of fall. Winter squash and pumpkins start to line the windows and shelves of Harvest's home. They compliment the natural decor of baskets and pottery, creating a warm cozy atmosphere. Exotic greens—kale, mustard, collards, arugula—and roots are grown and eaten fall through spring. They are cooked with rice and fresh deer meat, chicken or turkey. We have spent late mornings making broth and picking meat off of deer bones.

As the weather becomes less desirable to work in, Harvest retreats to the kitchen. Her kitchen becomes a palette for an array of squash dishes; pumpkin butter, pies, bread and candy. I am continually amazed at the creativity and life that Harvest brings to food. She has enthused me about cooking and canning. Her generosity is obvious to neighbors and friends who receive homemade canned goods and produce almost all year round. Canned salmon, spaghetti sauce with wild mushrooms, pickled summer squash and green tomatoes have often made it home with me.

Here in Hoopa, a little bit of spring creeps into the latter days of winter and becomes obvious when insect life starts to forage the newly blooming flowers. This time includes meticulously growing and nurturing seeds and seedlings. Almost all of Harvest's garden is grown this way. Each tiny plant is treated as the fruit bearing child that it is. Harvest gently tucks seedlings into her garden providing them with an abundance of organic matter below their growing roots.

They flourish and produce heirloom tomatoes including very tasty romas, large delicious old Germans and prolific fuzzy yellow peach tomatoes. Hot peppers join the tomatoes, in an assortment of colors and shapes. Heirloom potatoes, including Russian fingerlings and carolas have accompanied my favorite tuna salad, made with fresh basil, pickled winter squash and Light Lebanese summer squash. Parsnips, sliced thin, brushed with olive oil and broiled, have been described as "glorious," are also among my favorites. Harvest is not limited to her garden but uses her knowledge of wild food to add depth and texture to her meals.

Her kitchen has been a retreat where we have discussed many topics. Harvest is an avid reader and updates herself daily in the news. She became increasingly concerned over the rush of articles regarding climate change, crop failures and worldwide food shortages. Our daily conversations began to include ideas for having a sustainable food storage plan.

Harvest has called on a lifetime of knowledge, passed from many generations, regarding wild food, gardening, medicinal plants, and food preservation to share with the readers of *Food Security & Sustainability for the Times Ahead*. She is also committed to finishing, *One Day at a Time in the Garden*. In the meantime you can find more information about Harvest's garden routine here: <http://harvestsgardeningsecrets.blogspot.com/2006/01/simple-garden-routine-useful-for-bad.html> and links to more of her on-line articles on her web site: <http://www.HarvestMcCampbell.com>

Jessie Palmer
Hoopa, California

Acknowledgments

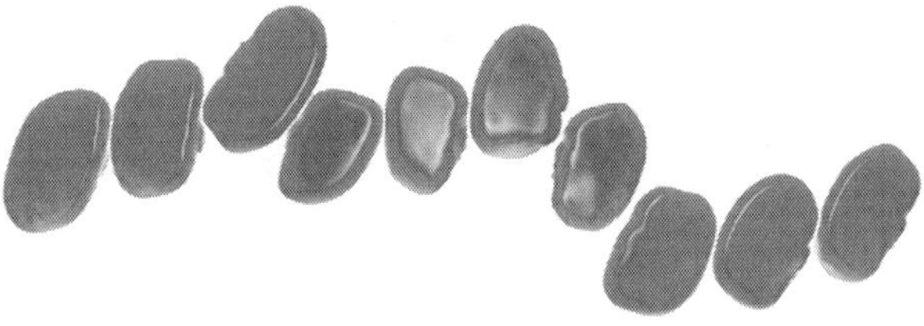

First, a big thank you goes to my young friend and assistant, Jessie Palmer. This book was her idea and our conversations helped give it shape. She also humored me by writing **About the Author**. Writing is not something she enjoys. She suffered over every word. This young lady shines in my eyes, much like I see that I shine in hers.

Terri Holtzclaw Reiser took a very rough draft, created out of passion and urgency, and orchestrated its conversion into a work worthy of being published. This is my first major work since a bad car accident, which left me with lingering brain damage. I cannot over stress the patience and diligence that Terri brought to this book. Terri, I hope you know how much I appreciate your hard work.

T'Uy'Tanat-Cease Wyss, who so graciously wrote the introduction, has been my distant sister in the on-going exploration of food, medicine, and sustainability. Her stories about growing up in an Indigenous tradition, completely surrounded by, in her word, a "megapolis," have kept me aware of the issues of the urban dweller, over a decade after I abandoned city life. The sharing of our stories and the teachings of our ancestors has nourished this narrative. Thank you so much Cease, I hope we get to talk story face to face someday very soon.

Sal Camarillo is my right hand man. Sal and I have a large and active news group, Northern California Native Events and News <http://groups.yahoo.com/group/ncanativeeventsandnews/>, to which he selflessly dedicates himself, even though he lives in Southern California and is a member of the Hopi tribe of Arizona. He always cheers me on and unselfishly applies himself to the tasks at hand. While I have been working on this book, he has had to pick up the pieces I put down, in order to keep the news group going. On top of this, he took a fine tooth comb to the manuscript and teased out mistakes that neither Terri nor I had found, even on several readings. Thank you, thank you, thank you, for all you do.

Kudos go to Kristen Freeman, and all the staff at Kim Yerton Memorial Library and Humboldt County Libraries, for their devoted work to the community and for the diligence applied to finding all the offbeat reading material that helps me attempt to understand this wonderful but imperiled planet we all call home. Where would we be without libraries? Visit yours today!

This book is part of an on-going conversation about the place we human beings occupy on, and our relationship with—our planet, our earth, our Mother. I have been informed by many thinkers, speakers, and writers, beginning with my grandmother, and expanding to encompass individuals of many different ethnicities and cultures. Names are important, but many evade me now. If you have informed this work, please know you are deeply appreciated. When we meet, or possibly meet again, I will thank you with my own voice and the touch of my hand.

I also thank you, Dear Readers. You who may have tossed and turned in uneasy dreams; you who may have read the on-going news of climate change and crop failures with trepidation; it is to you that I must offer my most heartfelt thanks. Those other Dreamers, the original Grandmothers of us all, heard your need, planted a seed, made sure it was passed to me, and here is another piece of the conversation about the transition before us. In a very real and fundamental way, without you, Dear Readers, this book would not exist. I hope it answers at least a small part of your need.

Last, but not least, I would like to acknowledge the ancestors, the sacred Grandmothers, and my own Gram. Without them I would not exist. I hope this meager offering does not insult their Dreaming.

All my relations,

Harvest McCampbell

Jessie Palmer
by H. McCampbell

Kristin Freeman
by L. Miller

Sal Camarillo
by J. Camarillo

T'Uy'Tanat-Cease Wyss
by S. Wyss

Terri Holtzclaw Reiser
by T. McKenzie

Bio Diverse Press

Our mission is to publish titles that will encourage bio-diversity in farms, gardens, urban areas, and open space; and that will promote practices, careers, economies, and life styles based on renewable and sustainable resources.

We are currently seeking queries related to our mission. If you are an established writer or teacher with a book idea, which will support families, communities, and businesses who are striving towards sustainable living and bio-diversity, please contact us. In addition to paperback books of at least 130 pages, we envision a series of full color books, 24 – 40 pages, rich with photos and accompanied by concise text. The following are some of the topics we would like to cover:

~Soap making with homemade lye
~Small scale vegetable oil production
~Hand processing cotton, linen, and other plant fibers
~Perennial staples
~Unusual tree crops for home or market gardens

We only accept queries by e-mail. Before contacting us you will need to set up a web site. (A yahoo group site is fine, and they are free. <http://groups.yahoo.com/>) For established writers, your web site should include a list of your publication credits and links to samples of your writing. If you are a skilled teacher, your web site should list your experience, qualifications, class schedule, and sponsors if any.

Once your web site is up, send us a brief e-mail explaining your book idea, with a link to your web site. If your idea is unique and can be fit into our production schedule, we will contact you for more information. E-mail us at: biodiversepress@ymail.com

Meanwhile, we have a few projects moving forward. Visit our web site at: <http://www.biodiversepress.com>. We hope to announce our up-coming books in the near future.

Recycle this Book

Every book, including this one, started out as carbon in the air. Trees sequestered the carbon in the form of wood. Young, quickly growing trees are the most efficient at sequestering carbon. When they mature and we harvest them for use as wood or paper, the carbon remains sequestered, and we can plant more trees to absorb even more carbon.

As long as this book remains a book, the carbon stays out of the air. But, if you throw it in the trash and it ends up in a landfill, it will rot in an oxygen deprived environment and much of the sequestered carbon will turn into methane and be released into the atmosphere. (Methane is another greenhouse gas, considered even more detrimental than plain old carbon.) Or, if you, or your solid waste management service, burn the book—much of the carbon turns into smoke and pours into the air. Recycle your book and keep the carbon out of the atmosphere.

When you are done with this, or any book, pass it to a friend, donate it to a library or school, give it to a used book store (where you can get credit towards another purchase), drop it off at a recycle center, or shred it and use it for mulch, add it to the compost pile, or feed it to the worms. That way you can be sure that the carbon sequestered by your purchase won't be squandered and released back into the air.

Many communities now have recycle centers and most of them accept paper of many kinds. If we can keep our paper products out of the trash, landfill, and incinerators we can reduce carbon emissions significantly. It is one small step we can all make.

Please recycle this book!

Index

A

aches and pains 66
acorn(s) 97
agricultural pollution 27
agricultural water 95
agricultural 11
agriculture 19, 23, 24, 81, 93
allergic reactions 66, 67
American Ephedra 66
anodyne 67, 69
anti-biotic 62
antidepressant 66
anti-fungal 62
anti-oxidants 48, 50, 60
antispasmodic 66, 67, 68, 69
anti-viral 62
aquifers 27, 37, 95
archery 77
arrow (s) 77, 106, 126
astringent 67, 69, 106
athlete's foot 68

B

bacteria 69, 90, 95
balance, nature 14
balanced diet 47, 48, 51
basic disaster plans 98
basket weaving 99, 116, 122
beans 36, 44, 47 - 49, 56, 123
  in a balanced diet 78
  storage 57
  sustainability 79
bedstraw 66
bee keeping 99
bees wax 35, 37, 40, 99
  bear country 35
beets 50
beneficial insects 86
berries 50, 57, 59, 79, 113, 129
birth control 99, 100
black beans 79
black turtle beans 56
bleeding 69
bloating 69
blood 66, 68, 69, 115
bones 48, 50
bottled water 44
bows and arrows 77
brain activity 112
brain cells 48
brainstorming 74, 93, 96, 97
bruises. 67
bug eggs 33, 40, 46

C

cabbage 89
calcium 49, 50
canned food 42, 46, 50, 79
  and sustainability 97
  clams & oysters 51
  fish & meat 49
canning 51, 54, 100, 101, 123
carbohydrate 43, 48, 78
carminative 67
carminative 69
carrots 86
catchment 27, 28, 94, 96
cayenne 60
cell walls 48
ceramics 103, 116

chicken 42, 49, 50, 122, 129
chili pepper 60
cholagogue 67, 68, 69
chronic congestion 66
cistern 27, 94, 96
citrus 59, 87
clams 51
cleavers 66, 68
climate change 14, 121, 132
agriculture 20
diversity 87
electrical service 46
fires 11
food supply 56
fossil fuels 118
news 130
pandemics 58
preparing 8
wild food & medicine 108
cob 105, 126
cold sores 62
comfrey 67
community 9
disaster education 74
food security 28
garden(s) 23 - 25, 85, 87
supported agriculture 24
complex carbohydrate 48, 78
composting 101, 107
condensation 36
congestion 60, 66, 67
constipation 69
container(s)
gardening 17, 23
homemade 17, 122
cord wood building 105
corn flour 86
cost of food 12, 23
cost of living 29
coughs 67
cramps 69
creek(s) 51
crochet 104, 116
crop(s) 105
adaptability 56
disruption 19
diversity 57
genetic diversity 56
prices 15
crop failure 31, 132
climate change 16
food reserves 26
food storage 23
immune system 58
insurance 31
news 10, 14, 15, 130
crop land flooding 37
CSA 24, 25, 80, 81, 100
cuts 62, 73
cyclone 19

D

dairy
community supported 24
regional production 28
decoction 66, 67, 68
dehydrate 42
dehydrating 90, 101
demulcent 67, 69
depurative 66, 68, 69
desert tea 66
desiccant 36, 101
diabetes 115
diaphoretic 66, 67, 69
dietary fiber 48, 49
digestion 67, 69
digestive tract 69

disaster 72
- community education 74
- electrical service 46
- emergency cache 84
- food storage 45
- insurance 31
- kits 74
- meals 32
- nutrition 58
- waste management 107

disaster plans 98
disaster preparedness 4, 84
disasters in news 19
disease(s)
- avoiding 48
- epidemics 16
- food shortage 58
- modern culture 115
- of plants 19, 20, 56
- organisms 100

diuretic 66, 67, 69
dock 68
dowsing 107
drinking water 44, 95, 124
drought 19, 23, 27, 29, 49, 120
dry beans 44, 47, 48, 49, 123
drying food 23, 56, 90

E

earthquake(s)
- electrical service 46
- emergency cache 82, 83
- food hazards 35, 37, 38
- regional risk 27
- storage containers 39
- transition 15

earth's balance 117

Echinacea 60
edible wild plants 50
eggs 24, 43
electrical service 46
elimination 48, 66
emergency water 44
energy
- efficient food storage 90
- electrical 46
- for manufacturing ammo 76
- healthy fat 48
- solar 127

Ephedra 66
ethics 38
expectorant 67, 68, 69

F

falling hazard
- food cache 36

farm(s) (farming)
- finding local 80
- forest 61, 87, 125
- loss of diversity 56
- organic 16
- products, regional 28
- sustainability 21, 23
- traditional 126
- volunteer 25
- volunteer opportunities 24
- water quality 94
- you can 124

farmers market(s) 80, 100
fat
- dietary 49
- nuts 43
- processing 52, 53, 54

soap making 104
fava beans 57
febrifuge 66, 67, 68, 69
female system 67
fennel 67, 70
fermentation 90, 106
fever 69
fiber 48, 134
arts 99
composting 101
dietary 49
plant 104
spinning 105
fire
cache 37, 82
California, recent 11
cooking 17, 72, 121
danger
considerations 72
containers for 39
hot wax 40
danger, regional 29
forest 79
news 19
pit (pottery and ceramics) 103
rendering fat 52
risk 82
salt substitute 63
transition 15
firearms 76
fire making 101, 102, 126
firewood 51
first aid 74
first aid kit 74, 83, 84
flax 49, 104
flint knapping 106, 126
flood(s) (flooding)
agricultural risk 120
cache 37, 38
Midwest 11
news 19
preparation 72
risk 29
root cellars 89
transition 15
warnings 10
floodplain 26, 82, 83
fomentation 66, 68
food buying club 80
food preservation
canning 100
drying 90, 100
old time 88
traditional 105, 106
fossil fuel 19, 118
fuel
emergency supplies 83
food prices 120
news 121
petroleum 28
wild fire 82

G

Gallium 66
garden (s) (gardening) 10
food security 85, 86, 87, 120
garlic 58, 59, 60
gas pain 69
glaciers 16, 26, 27
global warming 11
gourds 102
grain 24, 28, 36, 56
balanced diet 78
complex carbohydrates 48
cooking 123, 124
dietary flexibility 56
family budget 56, 80

fiber 49
high humidity 36
protein 49
sprouting 123
storage 38, 44, 47
sustainability 79
wild 77
Gram, grandmother
bio 13
Green World 18, 92, 116
insects 34
skills 17, 97, 96
stories 8, 10, 13, 116
teachings 14, 17, 132
grapefruit 59
greens 50, 77, 129
Green World 10, 12, 14
gun powder 77

H

haemostatic 69
hand dug wells 96
hazards 40, 84
physical, of stored food 38
to food 35
headaches 67
healing 67
healthy fat
energy levels 48
sources 49
heal wounds 69
heart disease
modern culture 115
heat 34, 37, 74
hemostatic 67, 69
herb(s)
basic information 68
birth control 100
books 71
calcium 50
essential 66
finding classes 64
general information 64
Gram 13, 17
mail order 70
medicine 108
preparations 68
safety 70
school 126
soap making 104
source 125
storage 65
wild crafting 70
herbal medicine 17
hide tanning 102
high blood pressure
modern culture 115
high energy food 43
homemade canned goods 129
hot peppers 33, 35, 60, 130
humidity 36, 45
hurricane 19, 35, 37, 38, 39

I

immune enhancing 60, 61
immune system 50, 58
Indian tea 66
infection 62, 63, 69
infusion 60, 66, 67, 68
insect eggs 40
insects 14, 31, 33, 36, 86
irrigation 26, 27
irritation 62, 73

J

jobs 29, 115
joints 66, 69
jojoba beans 54

K

Katrina 73
kettle 35, 44, 51, 53
kiln 103
knitting 104, 116

L

laxative 68, 69
lemon 59
light, effect on food 38
lightning 11
lima beans 57
lime 59, 129
liver tonic 67

M

masonry 105
meat 42, 49, 51, 52, 55, 57, 102
medicinal plants
  grandmother 17, 97
  local 64
  source 125
menopause 67
metal
  containers for cache 83
  depleted 19
  fire 39
  lids 37
  not renewable 77
  rodent proof 34, 35, 38, 40
  rust 42
milk
  mother's 67
  powdered 43
minerals
  dietary 63
  food sources 50
  industrial 19
  in salt deposits 63
  need for 48
  supplemental 59
mint 67, 68
Mormon tea 66
morning sickness 67
mother's milk 67
mucous membranes 69
mullein 67, 68
muscle tension 67

N

nerves 48, 67
nervous system. 66
nutritional balance 48
nuts 43, 49, 54, 87

O

obesity, modern culture 115
oil
  cooking 49
  for food preservation 106
  other uses 49

peak 8, 92
production, petroleum 26
soap making 104
vegetable 52, 54, 55, 134
olives 54
oil 130
Oregon grape 58, 61, 62
oven 52, 121
oxygen 92, 93, 135
rancidity 38
reduce, for food storage 54
reforestation 16
trees 87
oysters 51
oyster shell 50

P

packaged snacks 73, 74
pain 66, 67, 69
painful muscles 66
pasta 43, 46, 48, 79
peppers 33, 35, 60, 61, 130
permaculture 79, 87, 96, 126
perspiration 69
petroleum
and food sustainability 28
phyto-nutrients 48, 50, 60
pickles 79, 90, 97, 106
popcorn 45
pores 69
potassium 77, 101
potatoes
moisture 45
meat and 57
complex carbohydrate 78
winter food 86
storage 89
heirloom 130
pottery 103
poultice 67, 68
poultry 24, 55
power plant 46
pregnancy 62, 67
protein
emergency supplies 42
food sources 49
insects 34
powder 49
pumpkins 89, 129
purified water 51

R

rain 27, 28, 36, 83, 94, 95, 96
rain barrel 94, 96
rainfall
low 28
high 36
rainwater catchment 96
raw nuts 49
red beans 79
regularity 49
renewable energy 127
reproductive 66, 100
respiratory ailments 68
respiratory system 66, 69
rice 38, 39, 46, 56, 57, 80, 129
rice cakes 45
river 26, 27, 49, 51
root cellar 37, 89, 91
root crops 86
Rosa 59
rose hips 59

S

salt 62, 63, 64, 90, 106
sauerkraut 90
scrapes 62
seeds 103, 129
  Echinacea 60
  from food, growing 87
  garden 74
  garden, source 70, 125
  gourds 102
  peppers 61
  saving 103
  source, herbs 125
  source of vegetable oil 54
shellfish 51
shiitake mushrooms 58, 61
smoke house 90
soap making 103, 104, 134
solar energy 127
sore throat 62
soy beans 49
spasms 69
spinning, fiber 104, 105
sprains 62, 67
spring(s) 26, 51
  boxes 94
  development 96
  finding 107
  house(s) 89, 90, 91
  improve 94
  pollution 95
squash 86, 89, 129, 130
squaw tea 66
staples 11, 31, 56, 105, 123, 129
stick tea 66
stocking up 11, 79
stomach ache(s) 67, 68
storms 14, 15, 28
straw bale 105
supplemental protein 49
sustainable 14
swelling 67

T

tangerine 59
tap water 44
tax 29
taxes 29
tea tree oil 73
teeth 48, 50
textured vegetable protein 49
tincture 64, 68
tip the balance 20
tonic 66, 67, 68, 69
tool making 106
tornado 19, 35, 38, 39
traditional skills 126
tree crops 99, 125
trout 51
turnips 86

U

urinary 66, 69
urinary tract 69
urination 69

V

vinegar 53, 68, 90, 106
virus 62
Vitamin B 12 51
Vitamin B12 50
Vitamin C 59, 60

vitamins
food sources 50
general information 64
need for 48
preserving 90
vulnerary 66, 67, 69

W

waste management 107
water
assessment 94
bottles 102
car emergency kits 74
catchment 94
development 96
emergency 51
filters 44, 51, 95, 96
for cooling perishables 90
levels 27, 46
nuclear energy 46
quality 94, 95
regularity 49
resources 94
retention 69
shed 27, 95
sources 26, 27, 107
supplies 16
witching 107
wax
bee keeping 99
freezing 40
sealing jars 36, 40, 41
weather changes 19
weaving 104, 105, 116, 121, 122
weight loss 66
well(s)
dousers 107
hand dug 94, 96
long term water plan 51
polluted 95
pollution 95
regional water 27
source of contagions 45
supplied by aquifers 27
water source 26
well being 9
nutrition 48, 50
wheat, 56, 57
white willow 67
whittling 107, 121
wild crafting 70
wild food
abundance 77
classes 98, 127
emergency cache 83, 84
food security 79
Gram 17
nutrition 50
and medicine 108
previous cultures 23
willow 67
wood carving 107
wood stove 90
world food security 57
wounds 62, 69

Y

yams 50
yellow dock 68
yerba santa 68

Made in United States
North Haven, CT
10 November 2026

22095610R00080